E-QUALITY:
BRIDGING THE TOTAL QUALITY INVOLVEMENT GAP

To our parents
Sylvia and Cyril Levy
Lilian and Alan Shapiro

E-Quality

Bridging the Total Quality Involvement Gap

Gillian Shapiro
Paul Levy
Swasti Mitter

sussex
ACADEMIC
PRESS

First published 1996 by

SUSSEX ACADEMIC PRESS
18 Chichester Place
Brighton BN2 1FF, United Kingdom

Distributed in the United States by
International Specialized Book Services, Inc.
5804 N.E. Hassalo St.
Portland, Oregon 97213-3644
USA

British Library Cataloguing in Publication Data
A CIP catalogue record for this book is available from the British Library.

ISBN 1–898723 12 5

Copy-edited and typeset in 10 on 12 Helvetica
by Grahame & Grahame Editorial, Brighton, East Sussex
Printed and bound in Great Britain

Contents

Abbreviations and Glossary

action learning sets: A management development concept originated by Reg Revans in the UK. It is based on the idea that managers learn by doing and reviewing what they have done, and on providing opportunities for them to carry out this activity in a variety of different circumstances.

affinity diagrams: A brainstorming method used to help understand systematically the overall structure of a problem. By using words that express facts, predictions, ideas or opinions about situations or subjects not previously experienced, the affinity diagram method organizes the data into an easily understandable diagram that provides clues about the overall nature of a problem.

BT: British Telecommunications Plc.

best practice model: A model comprized of working practices, policies, mechanisms or initiatives drawn from one or more organizations that represent a proven successful approach to solving a problem or achieving an objective, that can be mirrored by other organizations.

bottom-up management: An approach to planning or decision-making which is based upon consultation with those at the bottom of an organizational hierarchy, as opposed to "top-down" approaches in which instructions and decisions come down from the top.

BS 5750/ISO 9000: The UK and international standards for quality systems, which outline to both suppliers and manufacturers the requirements of a quality-oriented system. They claim to be practical standards for quality systems which can be used throughout industry, identifying the basic disciplines and specifying the procedures and criteria to ensure that products and services meet the customers' requirements. The various benefits of applying the standards are claimed as the following: money is saved (because procedures will be more soundly based and more efficient); customers are satisfied (quality is built-in at every stage); waste is reduced and time-consuming reworking of design and procedures is reduced. BS 5750 was updated in 1987 through user experience and this revision is identical with the equivalent parts of ISO 9000 Quality Systems in the interests of international harmonization and international trade.

CENTRIM: Centre for Research in Innovation Management.

CGIL: Confedirazione Generale Italiana del Lavoro.

continuous improvement: There is no one definition of continuous improvement, as there is no one definition of Total Quality Management. However, continuous improvement is generally accepted as meaning a company wide process of focused and continuous incremental innovation.

DG-V: Directorate-General – Employment, Industrial Relations and Social Affairs, Commission of the European Union.

DG-XIII: Directorate-General – Telecommunications, Information Industries & Innovation, Commission of the European Union.

economies of scale: The reduction in unit costs of producing an item as the scale of production is increased.

economies of scope: Those economic advantages which firms may obtain through being able to service a wide variety of different market demands.

EC: European Commission.

EFQM: European Foundation for Quality Management.

EQA: European Quality Award.

FIM: Federazione Italiana Metalmeccanici.

glass ceiling: A term applied to the organizational barriers that exist, preventing women progressing to senior roles within a company.

involvement gap: The shortfall in success of many organizational approaches to Total Quality Management, associated particularly with a lack of employee participation and commitment to the management philosophy. This can result from the employee's lack of understanding of the values and objectives of Total Quality or from the employee's perception that they are undervalued within the organization.

ISO: International Standards Organization (Quality).

JIT: Just in Time (manufacturing); an approach to management originally developed in Japan, which emphasizes very low inventories, frequent deliveries by suppliers, operator involvement and quality awareness.

KTAS: Kjøbenhavns Telefon Aktieselskab.

lead time: The time taken to complete an activity.

MBO: Management by Objectives.

MET: Matra Ericsson Telecommunication.

OECD: Organization of European Co-operation & Development.

OME OTE: Greek Telecommunications Workers' Federation.

open learning: an approach to organized distance learning.

OTE: Hellenic Telecommunications Organization.

paired comparison: This management tool is used for gaining group consensus on the order of priority of a list of action points which appear to have equal importance.

positive action (PA): Refers to programmes within a company that are geared to augment women's opportunities by redressing gender imbalances in employment prospects and categories. The programmes entail evaluating the causes and impacts of gender inequality and endeavour to find means of correcting past imbalances, eliminating existing discrimination and promoting equality of opportunity between the sexes.

PTO: Post & Telecommunications Organization.

PTTI: Postal, Telegraph & Telephone International.

QIP: Quality Improvement Programme.

tacit skills: Skills and knowledge learnt informally whilst in a job role.

telecommunications industry: Refers to the separate industries that make up the telecommunications sector. In particular, the report concentrates on the equipment and service industries.

telecommunications sector: Refers to the aggregate of telecommunications industries. This includes the equipment and service industries.

top-down management: A method of disseminating ideas (e.g. for change), which starts at the highest levels of an organization and employs an iterative process of pervasion downwards through the hierarchy.

TQ: Total Quality.

TQM: Total Quality Management, a philosophy for applying quality control and management to every aspect of an organization's operations.

tree diagram: A diagram which shows the inter-relationships among goals and measures. The technique helps to think systematically about each aspect of solving a problem or achieving a goal.

UILM: Unione Italiana Lavoratori Metalmeccanici.

Acknowledgments

This book provides results of research which was conducted by the authors with the support of the European Commission. Thanks go to both Janet Hemsley of the Equal Opportunities Commission in Manchester and Antonella Schulte-Braucks of the Equal Opportunities Unit at the European Commission for their guidance and support throughout the project.

The ways in which companies are implementing Total Quality Management, the successes they have had and the problems they face, can only become the subject of contribution to knowledge and learning if those companies openly share their experiences. Therefore, our thanks go to the companies and individuals within them that participated within the research.

Gillian Shapiro
Paul Levy
Swasti Mitter

1

A New Approach to Positive Action Programmes

In a recent international survey of business Total Quality Management (TQM) techniques were shown to be used by over 90 percent of the respondents. Yet recent research also shows that very few companies adopting TQM are fully achieving their desired goals (A. T. Kearney, 1992). Lack of employee involvement, a prerequisite of successful TQM, has been highlighted as a potential reason for this shortfall (Shapiro et al., 1994)

This book, based upon empirical research carried out in telecommunication organizations in five European countries, is one of the first to attempt to establish a link between TQM success and equality. The research demonstrates a commonality between the goals of equal opportunities and TQM through the development of equality-driven involvement. The authors conclude that equality objectives are likely to be more effectively implemented if they are synchronized with overall organizational strategic objectives. Conversely, organizations adopting TQM need to place a greater emphasis on issues of involvement, which recognize the diversity of the work force. Without *integrating* the underpinning philosophies of equality and Total Quality, it is difficult to generate consistent levels of involvement throughout the work force. Such involvement is fundamental to the people-driven aspect of a successful TQM programme.

The European telecommunications sector holds a vital strategic position in any economy that relies on information-processing activities. In 1990 the European telecommunications sector had a turnover of 90 billion ECU. The sector also acts as a major employer throughout Europe, employing a high proportion of women. This book highlights the largely under-utilized skills and potential contribution women employees could make to Total Quality Management programmes currently being developed in the European telecommunications sector. It explains how the principle of Equality Driven Total Quality can extend equal opportunities policies and positive action beyond the traditional approach of gender-based equality to encompass the full diversity of a work force, and how the principles involved can be applied to other sectors. As such, the findings of the research and conclusions drawn are relevant to all those stakeholders in an organization who are concerned with increasing levels of involvement in Total Quality programmes, as well as making their equality programmes more effective.

The "involvement gap" has been at the root of industrial relations from the beginnings of business organization. The move away from a Fordist model of production towards more flexible forms designed to meet an increasingly changing environment has seen a growth in the amount of interest being taken in the field of organization design and development, particularly in the field of human relations. The findings discussed in this book herald an exciting new approach and a potential way forward for industrialists and academics to bridge company TQM and equal opportunity programmes, with the realities of a diverse work force. Current US literature in this subject area includes John L. Cotton's *Employee Involvement*, which concentrates on bridging the "involvement gap", and Susan E. Jackson's *Diversity in the Workplace*, which emphasizes the need for organizations to capitalize on employee diversity. However, E-Quality is not only amongst the first European book to argue the existence of a direct link between equality and quality, but it does so through a combination of validation through case study, synthesis into practical recommendations, and through a linking to the requirement of the European Quality Award.

Exploring the Equality/Quality Link

The objectives of the qualitative case-study interviews carried out within six telecommunications companies from five European countries were:

- to review the progress and approach of European companies to both equality and quality
- to explore the link between positive action/equal opportunities and Total Quality Management, focusing on the issue of the "involvement gap"

The link between equality and quality was explored through the concept of employee involvement – a theme found to be common to all of the company's guiding principles.

We set out to determine whether the involvement of employees, which underpins the TQM philosophy, and which is shown to be lacking in many companies struggling with their TQM implementations, may be increased through the development of a positive-action led, equality driven approach to Total Quality. Within the context of improving organizational competitiveness, the progress and approach of the companies towards equality and quality was reviewed:

- four of the six organizations had developed an equal opportunities policy; two of these companies had also developed positive action policies;
- of the two companies that had not developed equality policies, both companies felt that current practices reflected the values of equality without the need for an explicit policy;
- of the three organizations that established their policies between the mid-1970s and early 1980s, considerable progress had been achieved in this area.

Despite the improvements made by the companies in the area of equality, all of the companies continue to strive towards the objectives of:

- increasing the number of women in management;
- increasing training for diversifying women's skills;
- increasing the number of women in technical (and traditionally male-dominated) jobs;
- improving provisions to enable women to more easily combine work with home and family life.

In working towards the on-going objectives, the companies also continue to find themselves faced with barriers, some of which have been long-standing. They include:

- suspicion concerning the effect of equal opportunities on job security in the current economic climate and, in some cases, political climate;
- equality being regarded as a "Personnel" or "Human Resources" issue;
- lack of understanding throughout the organization as to what equality means;
- lack of resources devoted to developing equal opportunities;
- equality is seen as a low organization priority;
- cultural influences from society on the traditional role of women.

Five of the six organizations made considerable progress toward the achievement of TQM objectives. The remaining organization is currently considering the adoption of the TQM philosophy. However, the following concerns were expressed during the case-study work, highlighting the challenges that continue to face the companies in this area:

- TQM continues to be received differently in different parts of the organization;
- levels of commitment to the core values of TQM continue to vary within different parts of the organization;
- concern over how employee commitment and progress towards achieving TQM can be maintained (and in some cases, improved), was expressed.

Three major conclusions were revealed:

1 equality objectives are likely to be more effectively implemented if they are synchronized with overall organizational strategic objectives;
2 organizations adopting TQM will benefit from a better focus on the issue of involvement. In particular, the diversity of a

work force needs to be recognized, and TQM should be designed to bring out the best inherent in that diversity. Quality awards such as ISO 9000 and the European Quality Award should not be viewed as the end of the Total Quality road, but be assessed in relation to achieving long-term involvement, combined with continuous improvement;

3   a commonality exists between the goals of positive action/equal opportunities and TQM through the issue of involvement. Hence a linked approach, through an integrated equality-driven TQM philosophy, represents an opportunity for increasing the success of both TQM and equality policies.

The findings of the study showed that by integrating the practices of equal opportunities into the fabric of TQM, the goals of TQM and positive action can be furthered. As such, an integration would contribute towards the achievement of the organization's commercial objectives and can be regarded as a significant strategic innovation.

It is therefore the aim of this book to provide an overview of the stages companies have reached in their pursuit of the objectives of positive action. It also offers guidance on priority areas for future research, and modes of exchange of knowledge that could be undertaken in improving and harmonizing working conditions for women throughout the European telecommunications industry. The implications of the book's findings, however, extend beyond the gender issue. Indeed, it is our view that the book makes a relevant contribution to the broad range of equality issues as well as the field currently emerging within Europe of "diversity management".

Background to the New Approach

During the period November 1992 to May 1993, a pilot study was undertaken by the Centre for Business Research (now called The Centre for Research in Innovation Management – CENTRIM), with assistance from the Equal Opportunities Unit of DG-V (Directorate-General – Employment, Industrial Relations and Social Affairs, Commission of the European

Union) to explore the possibilities of a fresh approach to promoting women's opportunities in the telecommunications sector. The telecommunications sector refers to the aggregate of telecommunications industries; this includes the equipment and service industries.

This book summarizes the findings of the pilot study. It is envisaged that the results of this study will be relevant not only for formulating programmes in the telecommunications sector; but also for other sectors, where a substantial proportion of workers are women. In formulating a new approach to positive action programmes, the telecommunications sector is particularly important as it:

- has a large share of women employees in its workforce;
- represents investment in leading-edge technologies such as communication and information systems;
- contains companies that are committed to the Total Quality Management (TQM) philosophy;
- opens up possibilities of new working practices and locations, such as distance working and home-based working, that are relevant for women's career progression and the quality of working lives;
- offers the scope of learning experiences that are transferable to other sectors and relevant European Union countries.

The pilot project is formulated against this strategic position of the telecommunications sector, adopting innovative strategies. The initial investigation has highlighted the areas of research and action that will assist the companies to utilize women's skills by extending women's opportunities. The mode of the research has been collaborative, among the EC, the management and unions of the pilot study companies and the consultants, in order to facilitate a mechanism which in future years will redress the past gender inequality by promoting quality and quantity of women's employment, and *also* improve the companies' competitiveness in the global economy by eliciting greater involvement from women and men employees.

In the context of emergent management practices in the telecommunications sector, broadly described as Total Quality Management, this book indicates how and why innovative positive action programmes, if properly formulated, can provide power-ful tools for achieving corporate goals of competitiveness and profitability.

We also aim to provide guidance to policy-makers at national and European levels through discussion of the research results. Two policies in particular are highlighted in this book. The first is the structuring and restructuring of training and education programmes for blue-collar women employees: given the speed of technological and market changes, it is the older female workforce who will face the prospect of redundancies more readily. The second is in the direction of innovations in work organization and working time, such as tele-work, flexi-time, flexi-years, that allow women to have demanding cognitive jobs without sacrificing the quality of their domestic life: a necessary condition for breaking the "glass ceiling". (Glass ceiling is a term applied to the organizational barriers that exist, preventing women progressing to senior roles within a company.)

As chapter 2 illustrates, there is a marked paucity of relevant data at the aggregate level. It was difficult to obtain breakdown of employment figures in this sector by gender, either overall or in separate employment categories. In spite of the current discussion and debate and projections around the spread of tele-work in the European Union including in the telecommunications sector, there is very little knowledge about the extent of such work among women managers and other employees. By looking closely at the current practices of the chosen companies, the pilot study highlights certain trends and identifies areas for further work that will enable the EC to produce aggregate employment statistics, on the basis of figures obtained at the level of individual major companies. The pilot study also indicates how the new work organizations and work practices can be made compatible with companies' needs to "involve" all employees.

A major outcome of this book is the identification of areas of action for training and retraining. Women-oriented training programmes are likely to succeed when the management relates them explicitly to the needs of the company. The focus of the work, thus is two-pronged: Firstly, to place women's skills-acquisition in the context of the telecommunications sector's endeavour to reach consistent "quality", both in products and in service delivery. Secondly the book focuses on the issue of how to train management in enabling women to contribute effectively to the stated goals of the companies.

Positive Action – The Next Steps

Automation and subcontracting, features frequently arising from the emergent management philosophies, often are necessary steps that companies have to take to stay competitive. However, they may also imply a wastage of those human resources that could effectively be used to promote the long-term survival of companies. The importance of tacit skills of workers, including those of the blue-collar workers, is now widely recognized in competing trade blocks, especially Japan. The belief that under-lies the Toyota production system, for example, is that:

> it is only human beings that can have the ability for innovation; hence once a number of human beings decreases, as a result of automation or computerization, the built-in self-innovation ability of the workplace declines, no matter how effectively the automation is implemented. (Swasti Mitter, *Computer-aided Manufacturing and Women's Employment: A Global Critique of Post-Fordism*, paper presented at the Conference on Women, Work and Computerization, Helsinki, Finland, 30 June–2 July 1991)

The recognition of the value of human resources in the tele-communications industry is gaining currency in the European Union; and it is in this context that the concept of positive action is becoming an important strategic issue. In order to receive the maximum benefit from the potential of women workers, some of the companies are exploring the possibilities of retaining the existing women employees, as far as possible, by giving them polyvalent skills, and recruiting and retaining women employees with rare cognitive skills, as in the field of software programming, by experimenting with the hours and locations of work to meet women's specific needs.

Whilst the worthwhile achievements that positive action pro-grammes to date have made should not be ignored, they have, nevertheless been limited in their effectiveness of raising aware-ness and responsibility for equal opportunities throughout the organization.

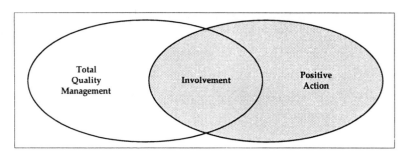

Figure 1.1   Positive Action Programmes as Approached from the Human Resources Department

Recent research, undertaken by the Price Waterhouse Cranfield Project (1991–1994) provides a possible reason for the limited effectiveness of equal opportunity programmes. It states that personnel departments within most European organizations play only a limited role in the formulation of overall organizational strategies. Yet, in the sample of this study, organization, implementation and responsibility for equal opportunities lies within the personnel department.

It is argued here that a consequence of the lack of involvement of Personnel in forming the strategic plan has been that, whilst awareness of equality as an ethical objective has been raised within organizations, it has proven difficult to synchronize the needs and goals of corporate organizations with the values and philosophies of equality.

In a highly competitive market, the European Union tele-communications sector can expand only by meeting customer demands for quality services and equipment. Thus, in this market-driven economy, the companies are forced to give priority to Total Quality Management in products, processes and service deliveries as a major corporate goal. Ensuring the success of the Total Quality in each of these stages, however, presupposes the *commitment* or *involvement* of the employees. The employees effectively contribute to the maintenance of quality only if they know the relevance of their work in the overall company objective. Also, the required involvement is possible only if the employees, including women employees, can have access to technical, marketing and business skills. Women, often with single outmoded technical skills, find it difficult

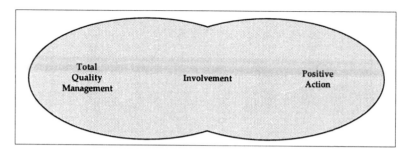

Figure 1.2   Positive Action Programmes as Formulated in the Context of Overall Management Philosophies

to contribute to such an exercise that ensures the criterion of Total Quality. Insofar as the companies exclude them, they lose the experiential skills of women that are vital for the continuous improvement of Total Quality.

Unlike TQM, the link between positive action policies and the total corporate goals has not yet been established. The ways in which human resource planning could contribute to the management of Total Quality has not been articulated explicitly. However, Figure 1.1 illustrates the unsatisfactory relationship between positive action and the overall management philosophy that may arise when positive action is approached from the Personnel or Human Resources department when, as is presently common, personnel has little, if any contribution to the formulation of the strategic plan. Positive action remains separate from the predominant organizational management philosophy thus excluding the full benefits of equal opportunities and employee involvement.

A potential conflict between distributive justice and organizational efficiency is likely to be less serious if positive action programmes are consciously formulated in the context of the overall management philosophies (Figure 1.2).

2

Research Methodology – Choice of Sector and Companies

The method of research followed directly from the aims and objectives of the pilot project. Investigation was focused on six large European Union telecommunications companies in order to delineate the factors that promote or inhibit positive action and equal opportunity programmes in the context of the current management practices. The research methods were also carefully selected in order to evaluate the gaps in knowledge that exist regarding employment and career patterns of women at the company level. It was envisaged that learning and experience at the micro level will assist macro-level policies particularly with respect to education and training at the sectoral and the European Union levels.

The research was geared at this stage to making a comparative analysis of six companies in five European Union countries; the areas of exploration, understandably, were the chosen companies' policies and practices regarding positive action, equal opportunities and Total Quality Management.

The European Telecommunications Sector

The telecommunications sector holds an important position in the European Community. It retains a strategic position in an economy that relies on information processing activities. The European telecommunications service industry had a turnover of 90 billion ECU in 1990 (*The European Telecommunications*

Table 2.1   European Community Telecommunications Trade Balance 1988 to 1992 (ECU million)

	1988	1989	1990	1991
Switching equipment	49	79	134	351
Transmission equipment	441	514	567	565
Radio-related equipment	38	14	77	140
Components	18	25	36	29
Terminal equipment*	(455)	(521)	(517)	(702)
Total	91	110	297	383

( ) indicates a negative balance
* including facsimile terminals

Source: Eurostat — COMEXT/DG-XIII

Table 2.2   Employment in Public Telecommunications Operators, 1990

Country	Telecom employment (000) 1990	Percentage of total employment 1990
Denmark	17.9	0.7
France	155.8	0.74
Greece	28.1	0.78
Italy	118.0	0.58
United Kingdom	226.9	0.94

Source: OECD, *Communications Outlook*, 1992/93 (1992).

Equipment Industry: The State of Play, Issues at Stake and Proposals for Action, Commission of the European Communities, SEC (92) 1049 final, Brussels 15 July 1992). Table 2.1 illustrates a worldwide telecommunications equipment market that amounted to about 383 million ECU in 1991. However, much of the growth is reflected in trade with developing countries and, in many product areas, the European Community falls behind the Japanese and the Americans.

Employment

The telecommunications sector acts as a major employer throughout Europe. Table 2.2 illustrates that the public telecommunications operators in each of the member states targeted for the purpose of this study account, in each case, for over 0.5 percent of total employment. (Employment data within private telecommunications operators was found to be unavailable.)

Table 2.3 Employment Growth Rates for Men and Women within the Transport and Communication Sector

Country	1983-1989: men	1983-1989: women
Denmark	4.4%	20.9%
France	0.5%	6.6%
Greece	-4.5%	8.0%
Italy	-0.7%	29.6%
United Kingdom	6.5%	37.9%

Source: EUROSTAT, *Labour Force Survey*, T. 43, 1989-1989 — Calculations DULBEA.

It is difficult to obtain a breakdown of employment figures by gender in this sector. However, by using the Transport and Communications sector as an indicator, one can safely say that the rate of growth of female employment, between 1983 and 1989, has been much higher than that of men, thus opening up new possibilities and career prospects for women (Table 2.3).

The positive aspect of this increase, however, is counterbalanced by the image drawn by impressionistic data that women remain concentrated in those categories of jobs where automation poses a threat of redundancy. The high concentration of women in part-time employment also enhances women's vulnerabilities in terms of career prospects and training.

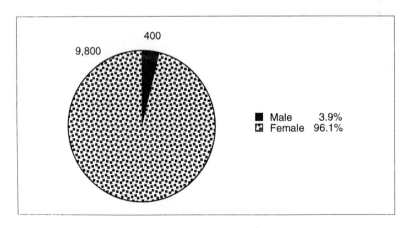

Source: Keynote (1992) *UK Telecommunications*

Figure 2.1 Part-Time Employment by Gender in the UK Telecommunications Service Sector, 1991

Whilst data on the number of women employed part-time within the European telecommunications sector overall is unavailable, within the telecommunications service industry in the UK, for example, the number of women working part-time is more than twenty times the number of men (Figure 2.1).

Competitive Environment

The telecommunications industry, in the 1990s, will be one of the main industries of the European economy. By the end of the century, telecommunications is predicted to account for about seven percent of the Union's Gross Domestic Product compared with three percent in 1988.

Historically, the various national post and telecommunications organizations (PTOs) which controlled domestic and international telecommunications were highly protected and had little incentive to improve efficiency, introduce new services or lower charges. They operated often with little apparent regard for customer needs. Additionally, because their foreign counterparts also enjoyed monopoly status, there was little opportunity to expand overseas.

However, the early 1980s saw the emergence of three powerful and inter-related forces: privatization; liberalization and globalization. Subsequently, the PTOs in many nations have split into separate post and telecommunications administrations, with the telecommunications business sold to the private sector.

Thus, privatization, deregulation, the changing nature of the market and moreover, emerging management philosophies such as "just-in-time", imply transference of jobs, especially jobs predominantly carried out by women, from the main manufacturing companies, to smaller subcontracting units.

Research Companies

The choice of companies was guided by a number of factors. Given the short period of investigation, it was deemed useful to explore the companies which are large enough to have national and/or international importance, open to the idea of positive action and equal opportunities in the context of TQM, linked to the research group through past research undertaken, and which are reasonably representative of the telecommunications sector, either in the production of equipment or in the delivery of services. The following companies were included within the study:

- Copenhagen Telephone Company (KTAS): Denmark
- Matra Ericsson Telecommunications (MET): France
- The Greek Telecommunications Company (OTE): Greece
- Italtel: Italy
- Ericsson Limited, UK (ETL): UK
- British Telecommunications plc (BT): UK

The method of selecting companies obviously has biased some of the results. To start with, the majority of the companies were favourably disposed towards the concept of positive action, equal opportunities and TQM. The challenge was to explore the possible ways of linking two concurrent philosophies and aims. The lessons learnt, therefore, need to be modified if and when they are extended to other companies in the European Union that are not yet so committed to positive action, equal opportunities and Total Quality Management.

Given the limited number of companies, the nature of investigation had to be primarily qualitative. In each case, the perceptions and opinions of interviewees cannot be stated as representative of the company as a whole. In a cross-company comparison of this kind, however, even the qualitative research poses certain problems as the culture of the country, its legislative framework and the social and political environment will deeply influence a company's attitude towards positive action and management philosophies. The research explicitly focused on the dimension of gender in formulating effective management practices; however, careful consideration has been given in interpreting these results for policy formulations at macro levels. The validity of experiences at a company level depends much on the "culture" of a country and hence cannot be always transferred to another company located in a different country. The commonality as well as the specificities of experiences were, therefore, assessed carefully.

Focus and Research Methods

The focus of the investigation, was centred around interviews carried out with relevant personnel from management, trade unions and with selected blue-collar and white-collar employees in the case-study companies. The interviews were semi-structured on the basis of indicative questionnaires that were flexible enough to cope with organizational diversities. The aims of the interviews were: to examine the initiatives companies have made towards positive action/equal opportunities, to understand the way the companies interpret TQM, to evaluate the prospects and problems the companies have faced in achieving their goals towards positive action, equal opportunities and TQM and to explore ways of augmenting women's opportunities that will enhance the company's continuous quality improvement.

The questionnaires were structured to evaluate the organizations' response to the implementation of both the TQM and positive action/equal opportunity policies. Generally, interviews with positive action/equal opportunity personnel were conducted separately from those who are in charge of Total Quality Management. In this way, it was possible to establish the presence or absence of the link between two corporate principles. The investigation aimed to synthesize such information that will be necessary for testing the hypothesis that the principles of positive action and equal opportunities, through increased employee involvement, can assist the companies in their pursuit of TQM.

3

Equality-driven TQM

The purpose of this chapter is to evaluate the relevance of positive action and equal opportunities for Total Quality Management. The definition of positive action, in this context, needs to be clarified. Positive action here refers only to women. It should be noted however, that its principles can be and are applied to other groups such as ethnic minorities and disabled employees. Approaches to equal opportunities and positive action vary from country to country. At one end of the scale companies develop equal opportunities policies as a minimum response to the law or code of practice in their own particular country. At the other end of the scale are companies employing positive action programmes as a means of driving through the equal opportunities policy and taking initiatives beyond legal requirements. Depending on the country and industry, a range of approaches can be found in between. Positive action programmes entail, on the one hand evaluating the causes and impacts of gender inequality, and on the other hand, endeavouring to find means of correcting past imbalances, eliminating existing discrimination and promoting equality of opportunity between the sexes, through appropriate policies.

It is possible to achieve a sustainable positive action programme only if such a programme is conducive to the long-term profitability of the company. As is the common experience, positive action programmes are often described cynically by the employees as the "flavour of the month", encouraged by the company only when the economic prospects are good or the company is shielded from competition artificially. The new approach in this project, thus, consciously and categorically places the positive action programme in the context of commercially-oriented management philosophies.

Our research was geared to assessing the validity of positive action programmes in the competitive strategies of the telecommunications companies. The current trend in the management practices is to ensure the retention or extension of market share with quick and efficient response to customer's needs. The relative shift of priorities, from production to deliveries, is a feature of the corporate organizations. There is a continuous pressure on the companies, not only to be cost-competitive but to be flexible and responsive to markets that are highly volatile. The quality and the variety of products and services often prove more effective than pure price-competitiveness as survival strategies.

In the telecommunications sector, as in many others, there has been a fundamental shift in the management practices and policies; whereby "the economies of scope" have superseded "the economies of scale" in importance. In these changed market conditions, organizations are responding to new economic and social environments that demand flexibility in the supply of products and services. The much needed flexibility has made it imperative for companies to move somehow from an old-fashioned traditional or "Fordist" model towards a more people-oriented, customer-centred philosophy. Telecommunications companies are adopting the philosophy, generally and often vaguely described as Total Quality Management (TQM) to address this shift. On the organizational level, it entails a shift from traditional division of labour between different sections and different categories of employment within a company, to a more integrated approach linking functions, skills and experiences within a company. The key to success is viewed in terms of "interfunctionality" between different sections of the company; so that efficient communications among employees could be established in order to improve the quality and timing of product and service deliveries. Quality is defined by companies in very many different ways . However, the policies essentially aim to advance, organizational flexibility, organizational ability to deliver high quality products, to respond rapidly to changes in demand and to be more cost-competitive.

The move away from the "Fordist" approach of the division of labour implies certain shifts in the management practices of telecommunications companies, most of all in implementing certain flexibilities in the existing bureaucracies. The quality is deemed most important; hence, much emphasis is given to the ability of the companies to receive certifications such as BS 5750 and ISO 9000.

The key to the company's success in achieving accreditation lies partly in changing the structure of the organization, replacing traditional "vertical" authority relationships with a matrix form of "horizontal" project teams. This democratic approach aims to improve communications among employees, a vital ingredient for ensuring quality in a quick response strategy. The companies engage in innovative practices, such as Quality Improvement Programmes, "Team Building" Programmes, Communications Programmes, Customer Care Programmes or Investment in Ready-made ('black box') technologies. The organizational approach, however, only partly guarantees the management of quality. The democratic approach heightens employee involvement, but many companies feel that the alienation of employees, a feature of "Fordist" organizations, can be lessened by opportunities and training for self-development through access to resource centres, discussion groups, action learning sets and such like.

Although the importance of employee involvement in achieving TQM has been acknowledged, organizations have experienced some difficulty in understanding its role in practice. The difficulty in understanding the specific role of human resources in Total Quality Management perhaps lies in the multi-faceted and multi-disciplinary nature of the field. The field is multi-faceted in that some see TQM as an organizational philosophy, some as a set of tools and techniques, others as a tool for strategic management, others as a means of managing human resources more efficiently and still others as some combination of these. These views have resulted in a wide variety of orientations to the subject and research on TQM can be found in a range of disciplines, including business management, management development, industrial psychology, job design and industrial economics, to name but a few. As in other subjects of study, such as organizational communication, there is yet to appear a satisfactory "unified theory of TQM".

Added to the variety of views interpreting TQM is the existence of Quality "gurus" whose orientations have influenced different companies in different ways. Some of the more famous of these:

Deming, Juran, Feigenbaum, Garvin and Crosby, have very different views about what constitutes TQM. In addition, Gurus in the broader fields of strategic management and organizational regeneration have also made significant pronouncements on TQM, such as Tom Peters and Peter Drucker. For a lay reader – this can create no small amount of confusion!

The research in this book suggests that many large organizations, such as those in the telecommunications industry are looking to a best fit model to act as a working definition of TQM. Many have turned to models such as ISO 9000 and, more recently, the European Quality Award. Such models present TQM as a framework or a system with a number of "ingredients" or elements. Progress towards TQM is proved by a company having in place a large number of these ingredients. In the case of the European Quality Award, the model also is represented as a process which companies can adopt. Though this has provided clarity on a European basis, lack of clarity about TQM still exists in many industries. Indeed, the whole nature of what constitutes a successful Total Quality programme is a source of much argument.

A. T. Kearney (1992) confirm the importance of "people involvement" in successful TQM programmes, but go on to document survey findings which suggest that a high proportion of firms engaged in TQM programmes pay lip service to human factors. Quality Awards, such as the European Quality Award stress the importance of "people satisfaction" and specify in moderate detail what is meant by this. Womack et al. (1990) give a detailed account of the lean production enterprise, with its emphasis on company wide problem solving and employee participation, extended beyond the organizational boundaries into the supply chain. Imai (1986) highlights the importance of such involvement in generating ongoing continuous quality improvement, while Crosby (1979), focusing on the costs of quality, demonstrates the need for employee attitudes which focus on problem prevention. For years, Deming, the guru of the quality world, has suggested the vital importance of employee involvement (1982), and this view has been supported by writers in the field of Total Quality Management, such as Oakland (1989).

The emphasis on people involvement has been given an

impetus also by the European Foundation of Quality Management (EFQM), whose European Quality Award for Total Quality is partly sponsored by the EC and whose specified standards are being adopted by European companies. The EFQM draws on many of the principles of the main TQM approaches of the past, augmenting them with increased emphasis on "people involvement" as well as stressing the need to look at "impact on society".

In its definition of TQM, the EFQM contains the particular aspect, "people management', which includes the following as key elements:

> "the company preserves and develops core skills through the recruitment, training and career development of its people."

> "the company promotes the involvement of all its people in continuous improvement and empowers its people to take appropriate action."

The strength of the EFQM definition is that it does make an attempt to link the total involvement of people in quality management with business success seeing "people satisfaction" as a key ingredient of "business results". In order to win the EFQM's European Quality Award evidence must be provided of:

> "the company's success in satisfying the needs and expectations of its people."

The new approach to positive action is thus set in the spirit of the current management philosophy. In an industry, where a substantial proportion of employees are women, companies are likely to benefit by adopting policies that will elicit greater involvement from their women employees. The research aims to facilitate a process whereby gender awareness could contribute to improving the organizational procedures that augment employee involvement and thereby Total Quality. However the recognition that positive action can form part of a total quality programme depends to a large extent on the type of approach which is taken towards developing TQM.

Foster and Whittle (1990) underline the need to understand the different root assumptions upon which many different approaches to TQM are based. Many approaches still develop out of hidden assumptions based around a Fordist approach. In such organizations, TQM is seen as a control mechanism: there is company wide involvement, but such involvement is imposed through a rigid control system. Hayes and Jaikumar (1988), in their overview of manufacturing, point to the obsolescence of such an organizational form in dealing with increasingly complex environments.

In the field of Continuous Improvement, Bessant et al. (1994), present a model which is underpinned by the use of involved teams of operators and staff engaged in a wide range of problem solving activities. Such a process is supported by a guiding strategy and infrastructure, but the process itself is driven by teams of empowered employees, using creative problem solving techniques.

Whittle et al. (1992) have identified four archetypal approaches to Total Quality in manufacturing organizations. These four "approaches" are useful in understanding the kinds of Total Quality Relationships which can be found concerning involvement at work. Visionary Total Quality (VTQ) focuses on the "message or vision" of quality. Its key design issue is one of control, including cost. Implementation tends to be a top-down approach, with emphasis on training and procedures, rather than tools, techniques and procedures. Planning Total Quality (PTQ) is more concerned with regulating processes, defining and managing boundaries, specification, information and measurement. Its implementation tends to be measurement and technology-driven. Learning Total Quality (LTQ) focuses on people, highlighting internal customer-supplier relationships. It can be viewed as an "involvement', participative approach. Implementation tends to be bottom-up. Transformational Total Quality (TTQ) provides an integrative framework, a "total" approach enabling organizational shifts between the three PTQ, LTQ and VTQ approaches. The TTQ approach focuses on management, its key design issue is innovation. Implementation is concerned with reframing, empowerment, partnerships & communication. The approach tends to be experimental. The distinct feature of TTQ is that it characterizes an organizational ability to recognize environmental changes, experiment with new behaviours and shift or transform the organizational form to meet new external pressures.

Therefore, it is only the TTQ approach which will facilitate the development of the dynamic, integrated organization which provides congruence between involvement and success. Its emphasis is on recognizing the need for "planning', "learning" and "visionary" elements at different times and in different contexts. The move towards the TTQ approach, requires for most organizations, a change in culture.

According to Schein (1985), culture has three levels. The first, *artefacts*, includes the physical and social environment and the outputs of the organization, e.g. written communications, advertisements and the way visitors are received. The second level, *values*, is less visible. It represents a sense of "what ought to be" often based on the convictions held by certain key people. Values are often debated in organizations and only when a particular value predominates, e.g. by demonstrating success, can it become a belief and ultimately a basic "taken for granted assumption. The third level of *basic assumptions*, is the least visible. This refers to the underlying assumptions which represent the taken for granted ways of doing things or solutions to problems.

Schein argues that cultures in organizations are formed which determine "how organization members perceive, think about, feel about, and judge situations and relationships" and these are based on a number of underlying taken for granted assumptions.

The dominant, taken for granted assumptions of senior managers in a commercial environment are obviously commercial, based on a competitive outlook. Much of the principle and practice of Learning Total Quality or of Involvement-based Total Quality arises from a recognition that such involvement can contribute to the companies' competitiveness and profitability. Thus, if positive action is to be fully successful and accepted by the boards of directors in the telecommunications industry it has to be compatible with the overall corporate objectives. In this way, positive action, as part of Total Quality Management, becomes a legitimate business strategy.

This chapter has shown how Total Quality Management Programmes are designed to deliver company-wide quality improvement. As such, they require the involvement, commitment and flexibility of every member of the organization. Many of the authors mentioned in this chapter discuss the need for "people involvement". Indeed, the word "people" appears to a major degree in today's management literature and people involvement has even been suggested to be a basic principle for leading organizations (Covey 1993).

The research in this book supports the view of McWhinney (1993), that "all creative people are not alike". Indeed, Lessem (1992) even points out that, not only are individuals different, but also that each individuals behaviour and attitudes to learning will vary along their individual biographical path. Organizations consist of diverse, overlapping groups which can be analysed along a range of dimensions (of varying importance in different situations): gender, ethnic background, education, politics, physical appearance, social background to name but a few. There is, of course, the danger here of over-simplicity and McWhinney suggests that "pigeon holing will stifle creativity". However, the oversimplified view of an organization being made up of a homogeneous group of employees as "our people" can create a number of difficulties in implementing TQM which are documented in later chapters of this book.

4

Stories from the Field: The Implementation of Equality and Quality Policies

The explanation of the methodological approach of this study emphasizes the importance of cultural, legislative, political and socio-economic differences between the organizations. However, some commonalities were found to exist between the companies concerning the business and organizational environment.

The Business and Organizational Environment

Each of the organizations are operating within the challenging and demanding environment of increased competition and economic recession, coupled with the opportunities presented by the opening up of the telecommunications market.

Due to recession, technical and organizational change, redundancies have been necessary, with the exception of OTE, in all the survey organizations. However, the threat of future job losses due to recession, technical change and privatization was envisaged within OTE.

Each of the organizations have undergone transition from electro-mechanical to electrical technology in their production process. Whilst each company has implemented cross-training initiatives to develop skills in the required new technologies, redundancies have occurred. Women, generally concentrated in blue-collar jobs, have been particularly affected by the technological changes.

Each of the case-study companies, with the exception of Ericsson (UK), have at one point, if not currently, been State run and owned. Whilst BT underwent transition to private ownership during the mid-1980s, other European telecommunication organizations are currently undergoing the stresses of such a transition. Both the Italian and Greek government are currently considering plans for at least partial privatization of their National telecommunication industry. Such moves are proving unsettling for employees within both these companies posing threats of increased job losses in the future.

Positive Action and Equal Opportunities: Summary of Case-Study Results

Implementation of Equality and Positive Action Policies

From the six case-study companies, four (British Telecom, Ericsson (UK), OTE and Italtel) had equal opportunity policies, two of which (Italtel and OTE) had also implemented positive action policies. Of the remaining two companies, KTAS and MET claimed that the organizational culture was one that enabled equality.

It was also suggested within MET, that the legislative laws governing equal opportunities within France were sufficient to ensure that the organization did not allow inequality.

However, it was noted by the Director of Personnel within TeleDanmark, that an equal opportunities policy would be implemented in the coming year. The implementation of this policy, it was stated, would then be cascaded down throughout the subsidiary companies, including KTAS.

Responsibility for Equality

Of the four organizations with equal opportunity and/or positive action policies, responsibility for meeting the objectives of the policies lay largely with the Personnel Directorate.

Within OTE, interviews showed that impetus to work towards equality came largely from the Unions. Overall responsibility was held within a committee consisting of representatives from Trade Unions, Management, Personnel and the Ministry of Labour. At corporate level, responsibility was held within the Personnel Division.

Within Italtel, the first impetus for equality and positive action policies came from the Trade Unions. These were met sympathetically from the then Chief Executive Officer, Maria Belisario. Overall, corporate responsibility for co-ordinating equal opportunities is held within the Personnel Division. A Commission exists, also at Corporate level, consisting of representatives from the three Trade Unions (UILM, FIM and CGIL), management, external researchers and experts. The Commission has responsibility for implementing equal opportunities and positive action initiatives throughout the organization. At Divisional level, "observatory" or monitoring groups exist to monitor the progress of these initiatives.

Within Ericsson (UK), the newly implemented equal opportunity policy was developed and is being implemented by the Personnel Policies Working Party. This group consists of managers represented from across the Divisions.

The Personnel Division at BT has been responsible for developing and implementing initiatives towards equal opportunities within the organization. Recently, in line with BT's commitment to "Opportunity 2000", the UK campaign to promote the number of women managers in organizations by the year 2000, an Opportunity 2000 manager has been appointed and responsibility for equal opportunities has been adopted at Board level.

Scope of Equality and Positive Action Policies

The stated organizational policies concerning equality for women within the companies were similar in scope. Each policy stated its commitment to raising the number of women in managerial and decision-making roles within the company, increasing awareness and responsibility for equality throughout the company and ensuring discriminatory practices did not operate in the areas of recruitment, selection, training, development and remuneration.

Table 4.1   A Summary of the Equality Initiatives Taken Within Each of the Survey Companies

Company name	Flexi-working	Training	Monitoring	Awareness raising	Other
OTE	little or no part-time working by women	in new technology	of position of women in the company	for women	
Italtel	part-time, flexi-work	in new technology	of position of women in the company & progress of EO and PA initiatives	for women	positive action research
Ericsson *	part-time, flexi-work				
BT	part-time, flexi-work & tele-work	in new technology, some EO training, management development for women	continuous monitoring of position of women & progress of Opportunity 2000	for women	networking of women & EO advisors
KTAS *	part-time				
MET *	part-time				

*   These are not the results of equal opportunity initiatives but already established working practices.

Positive Action and Equal Opportunity Initiatives

Whilst the scope of the equality and/or positive action policies were similar in each of the case-study companies, the initiatives that had been taken in working towards the equality goals differed to an extent (Table 4.1).

Part-time work was available to both men and women within each case-study company, including KTAS and MET that have no equality policy. However, few people within OTE work part-time hours due to low wage levels. Initiatives had been taken by OTE, Italtel and BT to specifically train women in the new technologies that had been implemented within the companies. Little evidence was found however, of specific equal opportunities training amongst the organizations, although some was found to have occurred within BT. OTE had established the mechanisms to take a snapshot at any one time of the position of women in the organization. Both Italtel and BT engaged in continuous monitoring of women's hierarchical positions. OTE, BT and Italtel had each carried out awareness raising initiatives for women, for example, encouraging women to apply for traditionally male jobs. Italtel are currently undertaking research into positive action in

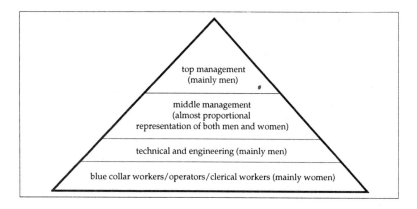

Figure 4.1   A Summary of the Employee Profiles of the Survey Companies, by Gender

order to identify best practices in this area. BT also operate a network of women and advisors in the area of equality.

Employee Profiles

In examining the structure of employment by hierarchy, function and gender in each of the case-study companies, a commonality in the position of women in telecommunication organizations was revealed (Figure 4.1).

(1) Middle Management With the exception of OTE, the number of men and women in middle management positions within the telecommunication organizations was fairly well balanced in terms of their proportional representation.

The gender split was slightly less well balanced in OTE at the middle management level. This is due to three dominating factors. Firstly, that job segregation between men and women was only abolished within OTE in 1979. Therefore, women within OTE have had less number of years within which to gain the skills to progress them to middle management levels. In addition, it was stated during interviews that few women were motivated to remain working for OTE for a large number of years or after, for example, starting a family. Finally, there are few women overall working within OTE.

(2) Top Management Without exception, each of the case-study organizations had very few women, if any, represented

at the top levels of management and in the decision-making positions.

(3) Blue-Collar Workers   In each of the case-study companies, the majority of blue-collar workers were women.

(4) Engineering and Technical   Another area where women were represented in very small numbers in each of the case-study companies was that of engineering and the more technical roles. For example, within MET, just over 15 percent of employees in top management and engineering roles were women. In OTE, women were not permitted to enter the technical field until 1985.

The organizations were also united in their demand for more technical skills. In MET, for example, the technical field was the only area where recruitment continued.

Skills Shortages and Skills Diversification

Each of the case-study companies predicted increasing requirements in the area of technical expertise, such as software programming and development.

However, few of the organizations had taken specific steps towards filling this demand by training to diversify women's skills in this area, or by specifically encouraging women to apply for these types of positions.

Positive Action and Equal Opportunities: Future Goals

Each of the four organizations with equal opportunity and/or positive action policies had aims to improve their moves towards equality in the future by increasing the number of women in management, increasing training for diversifying women's skills, increasing the number of women in technical and traditionally male job roles, increasing organizational wide awareness and responsibility for equality, and improving provisions to enable women to more easily combine career and family.

Barriers to Positive Action and Equal Opportunities

A number of barriers to the achievement of the above stated goals were highlighted during interviews. A major barrier was suspicion concerning the effect of equal opportunities on job security in the current economic and in some cases political climate. Linked to this was the danger of equality being regarded as a Personnel issue as well as a general lack of understanding throughout the organization as to what equality means. Added to this was the barrier of a lack of resources devoted to developing equal opportunities. Finally, cultural influences from society on the traditional role of women were also a potential barrier to achievement of goals.

Total Quality Management: Summary of Case-Study Results

All of the companies included in the study were, to a greater or lesser extent, proactively addressing the issue of quality management within their organization. In one or two cases companies were several years down the road of a TQM programme. In other cases, the programme was relatively recent and, in one case, a quality programme was at the planning stage.

Impetus towards Total Quality

TQM was seen by the survey companies as a way of moving the organization out of a traditional bureaucratic phase of operation towards a more dynamic, commercially responsive business. As a philosophy, TQM was seen as an integrative force, cutting across traditional organizational boundaries and directing the company's focus more towards the external customer.

In many cases a more overriding impetus towards Total Quality was the shorter-term goal of achieving the international quality standards ISO 9000/4. In several instances it was suggested that, although ISO 9000 was a useful starting point, the organization had overfocused on the procedural element of this standard to the detriment of the softer aspects of TQM such as involvement.

Organizational Values for TQM

A number of common values driving Total Quality (TQ) were identified. These were varyingly expressed in terms of values which focus on satisfying the customer; values concerned with continuous quality improvement, values which stress the importance of teamwork, values which stress professionalism and pride of work, and values which emphasize the importance of individuals' contributions.

The final area provides fertile ground for improving involvement at work. However, in many cases, it was stressed that the softer values such as involvement had received a lower priority from senior management who, in the short-term recessionary climate, remained unpersuaded about the importance of involvement and more concerned with cost reduction and profitability.

Organizational Features of TQM

However, common to virtually all organizations in the study were a number of organizational features which were underpinning the initiatives being taken towards TQM. These included a steering group at senior management level responsible for directing the programme and cascading the vision of TQM; senior and middle management involvement in identifying areas for quality improvement which contribute towards business objectives; quality improvement teams aimed at generating improvements in a range of areas, sometimes within functions, sometimes across functions. Typical projects would focus on defect reduction, problem identification and solution and lead time reduction. Teams would be led by a facilitator and would be trained in relevant tools and techniques.

Training for TQM

Common themes in training were identified as being focused on training in the goals of TQM and how it fits into the company's strategic vision, training in tools and techniques for quality improvement underpinned by training in teamworking (including training for facilitators and team leaders.)

Training would generally occur over a day or two, would involve working in a team, and would be supported by a training manual of some kind.

In several cases, training had only been given to those working directly on improvement projects. However, in almost all cases the companies had plans to give all employees a basic training.

TQM Tools and Techniques

The key TQM processes were quality improvement teams using tools and techniques working on improvement projects aimed towards improving business performance. Examples of tools common to most of the companies were: problem identification tools, problem analysis tools, problem-solving tools, and group working tools.

Benefits and Problems of TQM

Some of the benefits of Total Quality Management for the organization that were cited included a much more responsive organization (both internally and externally), improvements in service and product quality, profitability, and an improved interest in work through teamworking and increased skills.

As the companies moved away from the phase of bureaucracy towards a more integrated form they experienced some organizational changes (Figure 4.2). These shifts support some of the more general literature available on the emerging industrial paradigm (Bessant, 1991; Lessem, 1990), which describe a paradigm shift occurring towards more integrated forms of organizational design.

Despite the progress made towards TQM, a range of problems had been experienced in the pursuit of Total Quality, many of which relate directly to involvement issues. They can be analysed under the broad headings of senior management commitment, TQM values, TQM Organizational framework, and TQM and involvement.

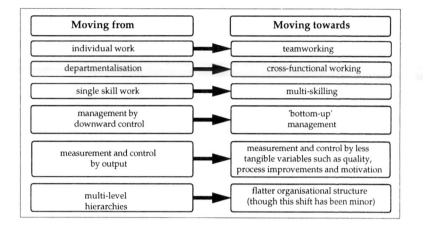

Moving from	Moving towards
individual work	teamworking
departmentalisation	cross-functional working
single skill work	multi-skilling
management by downward control	'bottom-up' management
measurement and control by output	measurement and control by less tangible variables such as quality, process improvements and motivation
multi-level hierarchies	flatter organisational structure (though this shift has been minor)

Figure 4.2 Organizational Changes Experienced Illustrating How the Case-Study Companies are Becoming More Integrated and Less Bureaucratic

(1) Senior Management Commitment A common problem identified was the role of senior management. In some cases it was felt that TQM was only being valued at a senior management level as a short-term way of reducing cost or of obtaining ISO certification. It was felt that some members of senior management did not fully understand the purpose of TQM and the role of involvement in it.

(2) TQM Values A number of problems concerning TQM values were identified. In some cases, it was felt that the values had not been well communicated and that awareness was piecemeal across and down the hierarchy. Some interviewees identified a conflict between what they felt to be senior management values and the values of the rest of the organization. In particular it was felt that senior managers over-emphasized the cost saving element as a value whilst giving less emphasis to such values as "we respect each other" or "we value our people". It was often stated that the values were "too ideal" and unrealistic; they did not really reflect the organization's mission in an increasingly harsh and competitive environment where job losses and cost cutting were realities to be lived with each day.

(3) TQM Organizational Framework A number of apprehensions in relation to the organizational framework for TQM were

identified. Firstly, the uncertain economic climate, together with deregulation and liberalization created uncertainty within some organizations concerning where TQM was going within them. Secondly, many of the organizations had experienced regular restructuring which confused the organization of TQM. Thirdly, because of a heavy focus (within some companies) on ISO 9000, much of the organization was geared around the achievement of this standard which had led in some cases to the development of more bureaucracy in different parts of the organization. Also this standard does not significantly recognize involvement as a key area and this had undermined efforts to change some of the organizations in a way which would encourage more participation at all levels.

(4) TQM and Involvement   The companies had all recognized the importance that gaining commitment to and full participation in TQM played in their success and had recognized that quality awards such as ISO 9000 and the European Quality Awards (EQAs) were only part of TQM and not the whole process. The European Quality Award was seen, however, as a particularly useful award to achieve as it focuses quite heavily on involvement, identifying "people satisfaction" as a key driver of Total Quality. Despite recognizing the importance of involvement, in practice it was found that the softer values named such as involvement had received a lower priority from senior management who, in the short-term, recessionary climate, remained unpersuaded about the importance of involvement and were more concerned with cost reduction and profitability.

Total Quality Management: The Involvement Gap

All of the companies were experiencing problems concerning gaining total involvement which were seen as undermining the overall TQM effort. We have named this problem as the involvement gap. That is the shortfall in success of many organizational approaches to Total Quality Management, associated particularly with a lack of employee participation and commitment to the management philosophy. This can result from the employee's lack of understanding of the values and objectives of Total Quality or from the employee's perception that they are undervalued within the organization. A number of themes emerged from the interviews concerning the implementation of TQM and the involvement gap.

(1) Business Climate   In virtually all of the companies in the study, there had been a significant number of recent job losses due to technological change and restructuring. This created a number of involvement issues in relation to making TQM work:

- people did not feel as committed to the organization, in some cases because of the way the company had treated loyal employees, for example, in making redundancies;
- people felt insecure in many cases and did not feel secure enough to make improvement suggestions which might in some way marginalize their position;
- an overfocus on the short term made it hard for people to commit themselves long-term to the organization or its TQM programme;
- the short-term focus on rationalization and cost reduction created confusion between this short-termism and the longer term values of TQM.

Overall, interviewees were unable in some cases to relate the goals of TQM with the goals of their organization and their own personal goals. It was felt that the business climate was creating a Planning Total Quality (PTQ) approach which focused too much on short-term measurable results. This was reinforced in some companies by the performance appraisal system which stressed the achievement of short-term cost reduction targets.

(2) Lack of Senior Management Understanding   In relation to the problems concerning the business climate, it was felt that short-termisms on the part of the board was undermining TQM, and that involvement had a low profile. In one of the companies, TQM was only being selectively used, and there were no mechanism at all for gaining total involvement.

(3) Staff/Line Division   Lack of involvement of staff in several organizations led to a situation where, in general, involvement was focused on the production lines and at the customer inter-face, and the support departments were neglected, though, in many cases, they represented a significant overhead cost. It is often in the support departments where many women are to be

found working, and, therefore such an approach, has an impact on equality of opportunity in TQM.

Lack of Equality of Opportunity

A number of issues were identified during the case-study interviews that indicated that the values and objectives of positive action and equal opportunities had not been taken into account in pursuing TQM policies. The emerging issues included the following:

- selection of team leaders and facilitators often came directly from the traditional hierarchy thus reinforcing any previous inequalities in place;
- little or no evidence was found of mechanisms to support flexi-working or TQM team meetings geared towards meeting the needs of people working at home or working part-time;
- in some cases, part-time workers had a lower priority attached to them in terms of involvement;
- TQM training materials were not put through an equal opportunities process (though it is difficult to know if this has had any negative impact);
- many employees working directly at the customer interface, such as receptionists, were women, and had shown the most enthusiasm and commitment towards TQM. Those further back in the organization, in more traditional technical departments had been less enthusiastic;
- little or no evidence was found of an attempt to build equal opportunities into the fabric of TQM although there was some recognition that there was a possible link between the increased involvement this might achieve and TQM success.

5

Case-Study Results

The results of interviews carried out within each of the chosen organizations reflect the different stages of implementation of positive action, equal opportunities and Total Quality Management policies within the survey companies. Thus, although presented in a common framework, the structuring of case-study results reflects differences in emphasis and priorities given to TQM and positive action by different companies. It should also be noted that, interviews were undertaken with only a small sample of personnel from each company. Parts of the data, therefore, represent the opinions and perceptions of interviewees and cannot be taken as representative of the organization as a whole.

The results of interviews relating to equal opportunities and positive action are presented first, followed by the results of interviews relating to TQM. "The Involvement Gap" section, at the end of each case study, contains an analysis of the perceived shortfall in linking positive action with TQM policies. The section likewise indicates some tentative measures for synchronizing the values and practices of positive action and TQM. The conclusions and recommendations drawn from the study are presented in chapter 6.

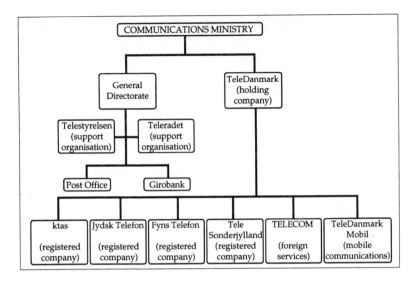

Figure 5.1   The Structure of Telecommunications in Denmark

Copenhagen Telephone Company (KTAS)

KTAS: Background Information

KTAS has been in operation as a telephone company for 111 years. In that period the company has undergone several periods of technological and organizational change. The past two years have also witnessed a change in the organization of the Danish Telecommunications Sector. As a consequence, on March 1 1991, KTAS and the other Danish telecommunication companies changed from being an independent limited company to a 100 percent owned subsidiary of the holding company TeleDanmark A/S. Figure 5.1 illustrates the structure of the Danish telecommunications sector and where KTAS is situated within this. Each of the subsidiary companies are geographically divided. KTAS has 1 300 000 subscribers.

The Danish telecommunication industry is able to claim that it has one of the best functioning telephone systems (in terms of quality of service) in the world (according to 1990 Organization of European Co-operation & Development (OECD) international statistical analysis) and is able to offer one of the world's cheapest telephone service. Employing about 7500 staff, KTAS represents a significant force in its regional area. However, due to external competitive demands, as a result of the European liberalization of the telecommunications market, KTAS faces fundamental structural changes. In preparation for such changes, one of the main goals of KTAS is to improve the quality of both its products and services.

The number of employees within KTAS today totals around 7500 compared with 7 680 in 1991. A little over 4500 of these employees work within administration and nearly 1000 within the area of service telephone.

KTAS' market is geographically limited. The company is the largest but, since liberalization came into effect in 1992, not the sole supplier of all terminal equipment such as telephones and private exchanges. It is the sole supplier of physical wire capacity and the sole basic carrier of services within its own company geographical area.

Faced by the challenges of liberalization, KTAS intends to become internationally competitive whilst maintaining its present services and equipment. Interviews with KTAS were carried out with management representatives, operatives and the Director of Personnel at the holding company, TeleDanmark.

KTAS: Corporate Approach to Positive Action and Equal Opportunities

Within KTAS at present, no corporate policy on equal opportunities exists. Interviews showed that there is the perception that women are encouraged to progress their careers within the company. However, there is also the perception that certain areas exist within KTAS where measures could be taken to ensure equality is in operation. It was stated that:

> "It's a little more difficult for women to qualify for jobs in some parts of the company. It's still a small problem, not domineering, but we would like more women to come into the company."

The majority of interviewees felt that overall, equality existed within KTAS. Some examples were given of areas of employment, such as field technicians, where it was felt that, it was difficult for women to be accepted within these roles due, in part to its traditional male history. However, this situation was reported to be gradually changing.

In response to questions concerning promotion within KTAS, it was revealed that it may sometimes be harder for women than men to progress their careers:

"Women need to be better than men to advance."

Reference was also made to the "male" or "harder" management style (such as an authoritarian style) that some interviewees believed individuals needed to show in order to progress within the organization. It was felt that some women may lose their important "softer', "feminine" skills (such as listening and a participative management style), in progressing through the company due to the company's "macho" or male nature.

"You need 'elbows' to progress."

"They (women) have to be able to fight (in order to progress)."

Despite references to "male" skills, recent examples were given of changes in this trend and value being increasingly attributed to "softer" skills being present in both male and female managers. Interviewees suggested that awareness training of the value of different management skills together with specific training for women in traditional male dominated functions would both help further the professional development of women within KTAS.

The holding company, TeleDanmark are currently planning a general management programme which will implement an equal opportunity policy. It was stated that this will be cascaded down to each of the subsidiary companies within TeleDanmark. The decision to implement such a policy in this programme is a result of recognition at corporate level that certain functional areas remain dominated by men and some by women. The policy will aim to redress the balance in these areas and ensure that the best use is made of skills in all areas.

The impetus within TeleDanmark to implement an equal opportunities policy came, in part from the recognition of the gender imbalance within certain functional areas.

Whilst the balance of male and female managers within KTAS is almost equal, with just under 60 percent of male middle managers, the picture at the top of the organization is less well balanced. Women make up just under 20 percent of top managers at KTAS. In addition, little over 14 percent of women are present within the specialist technical engineering side of the company. In contrast, women predominate at the blue-collar level and just over 75 percent of administrative staff are women.

Examples of gender dominated areas exist within sales, where between 80 percent and 90 percent of staff are women and the technical area where only 4 women are employed out of some 1000 to 1200 employees.

Despite the fact that KTAS does not have a formal equality policy, opportunities exist within KTAS for part-time working. In addition, both men and women are able to work flexible hours.

KTAS: Positive Action/Equal Opportunities – A Summary

The general picture drawn from interviews within KTAS showed that whilst the company regarded itself as having a culture that reflected equality, some employees felt the existence of the imbalance in the number of men and women within some areas of the company.

This issue is currently being addressed by the holding company, TeleDanmark, who plan to introduce an equal opportunities policy in the coming year which will then be cascaded down to the subsidiary organizations. Whilst evidence was found that emphasis in the past had been laid upon the importance of "harder" management skills in order to progress within the organization, it was the feeling amongst interviewees, that this trend was now changing. Increasing value is currently placed on the development of "softer" management skills in both men and women.

KTAS: Corporate Approach to Total Quality Management

Interviewees described KTAS in the past as a "traditional" company, "bureaucratic and stable". Today, the organization is characterized as "as good as a private company", less stable and less bureaucratic. TQM was introduced within KTAS relatively recently in the early 1990s. The main targets of TQ are: cost reduction, time reduction, defect reduction, and improved customer service. According to its Annual Report (1991):

> "One of the main goals of KTAS is to improve the quality of both products and services."

The report also underlines the emphasis on customer-driven quality: "Over the last year a special effort has been made to satisfy customer demands for shorter delivery times in connection with establishing subscriptions and when telephones have to be moved. This effort has been so successful that more than 98 percent of all tasks were carried out on or before the agreed date. In order to call attention to this remarkable service improvement KTAS initiated a campaign under the slogan 'When you move, KTAS establishes your phone connection from day to day'."

Particular strengths identified by interviewees also suggested some underlying values which, though not explicitly stated, were, nevertheless, present. These included: high skill levels, craftsmanship, professionalism, high educational levels, and flexibility/ability to change.

KTAS was once described as: "a place where you could have a job for life." Though this is still the case as far as some of the interviewees were concerned, they acknowledged that this is now much more dependent on individual's taking responsibility for their own work. Indeed, a key cultural change in the organization has been the shift in responsibility from the company to the individual. This is viewed as a step in the right direction and a step which is conducive to a TQM problem solving environment.

The culture was described to have changed in recent years to a more private company type one, focusing very much on customer needs. Much of the current culture was geared towards seeking to satisfy customers. It also contained a certain level of frustration resulting from a lack of communication and co-ordination between and across functions. Some functions were very tightly organized, introverted, and could be described as "cultural islands", whereas others were attempting to integrate far more with the whole organization. The lack of co-ordination and communication in some areas was seen to impact on customer service in some cases. For example, as one interviewee pointed out:

> "We have all the know how to get the job done, but don't always seem to have the capability to do it in the right place at the right time."

This problem is currently being addressed and an attempt is being made to emphasize a culture which puts the customer first. As one interviewee pointed out:

> "When we install a line, the customer must be able to use it 100 percent of the time. If we have to shut the line down, we must talk to the customer first, but we must avoid the disconnection if at all possible. It has been found that 750–800 of disconnections can be avoided in some way."

From a TQM viewpoint the culture was identified by many as procedure based, geared strongly towards ISO 9000, which did not fully reflect the "people" issues which TQM needed to address.

A range of channels for making suggestions for quality improvement within the company exists. There is a suggestion committee where an employee can describe their suggestion and send it in to the committee. An interviewee commented that this process is not always easy for a technician to follow as they sometimes experienced problems with describing their ideas in writing. One interviewee pointed out:

> "I am sure a lot of these suggestions do not come to the right place because some people are not so good at drawing it or writing it."

Further to this, at the local level, within group meetings suggestions can be made.

The main organizational mechanism for Total Quality are quality project teams. The quality project groups meet and discuss quality issues focusing on ways to meet the TQ targets of cost reduction, time reduction, defect reduction, and improved customer service.

This is currently viewed as working well with examples of significant improvements and cost savings being made in some areas. However, it was also pointed out that time was a limiting resource. People needed more time made available to work on TQM projects and often the day to day pressures of the job reduced the project team as a priority. It was felt that providing more time could potentially have significant longer-term benefits in terms of individual involvement. As one interviewee stated:

> "once individuals see suggestions work as a group they will begin to develop suggestions as individuals. By starting in groups people will develop confidence to make suggestions."

The key measures of success at KTAS were identified as: cost savings, time, quality improvement, and customer satisfaction.

It was felt by many that current prevailing economic conditions were forcing senior management to focus largely on cost.

Tools for quality improvement include use of a range of standard tools in the areas of: problem identification, problem analysis, problem solving, as well as group dynamic processes such as brainstorming.

Many positive comments were recorded regarding the quality of the TQM introductory training, about its presentation and delivery. A consultancy company was used to develop the training materials covering tools and techniques.

One challenge for the company is the next level of training and how to maintain the impetus for Total Quality in the future. The extent to which individuals or groups actually use the tools and techniques as part of their project team work is not accurately known. However, it was suggested during the interviews that the tools and techniques were used, though to varying degrees across the organization.

KTAS: The Future Challenges of TQM

A number of issues were identified during the company interviews which, it was stated, posed a challenge to the continued success of TQM within KTAS.

Firstly, long-time members of the organization find it, in many cases, harder to accept the messages of Total Quality and, particularly, in some technical areas, the focus is still on product quality and technical specification, sometimes to the detriment of the customer, e.g. taking a long time and effort to get a job right even if it means the customers telephone line is cut off for a long time. This issue is being addressed.

Added to this, a view in some parts of the organization expressed was that Total Quality means 95 percent quality and not 100 percent.

It was also discovered from the interviews that many members of the organization are so busy, often doing overtime, that they do not have the time to be "proactive" in the way that a Total Quality approach requires.

Several interviewees described the culture as "legalistic", where obeying the rules from above was a priority. Rules were there to be followed, not questioned. This potentially inhibited proactivity in problem identification and solution. As one interviewee pointed out: "we don't try to change the order of things, even if things are wrong."

It was also suggested that some leaders in the organization, particularly those who have been at KTAS for a number of years, feel that their power base and knowledge is being taken away from them and, therefore don't fully engage in the TQM values and activities. Some of them feel threatened by this. Generally, it was felt that involvement in TQM at KTAS was patchy at the level of day to day commitment. People were united on the goals of the organization and on what TQM was trying to achieve. However, the level of TQM commitment depended on the extent to which "older values" had been shaken off by the training, the style of local TQM leaders or champions, and the extra time available to engage in TQ activity.

With the analysis of the KTAS interviews and in light of the above stated challenges that were identified as now facing the continued success of TQM, it is suggested that KTAS could take the following action in order to offset the identified challenges.

There is clearly scope to take specific action to gear training and communication of TQM values towards specific concerns and needs, of longer-term members of the company, that is those who joined the organization when its culture was very different.

The important issue of Time also needs to be addressed, particularly in areas of the organization where the nature of the work puts strong time pressures on individuals and departments, if they are to fully engage in TQM problem solving.

In relation to the TQM programme, the impact of TQM on the organization as a whole, on power relationships, changing roles, and shifts in knowledge base might be better identified. Linked to this, many of the interviewees stated that there is a feeling that TQM is equated with ISO 9000. The organization needs to begin to look beyond ISO 9000 now, in order to ensure success of TQM in the future. ISO 9000 may prove a limiting factor in the long-term if the focus remains narrow.

KTAS: Total Quality Management – A Summary

Since the introduction of TQM within KTAS in the early 1990s, the policy has progressed well. With the use of TQ tools, techniques and measures, it has reaped the benefits of cost reduction and increased standards of quality for KTAS. The change in management philosophy has also been accompanied by a shift in the culture of the organization. Individuals now take responsibility for the quality of their own work and the overall success of the organization. The pertinent issue currently facing KTAS is how to maintain continuity in the improvement TQM has made to date and ensure continued commitment to the values of TQ from all employees.

KTAS: Positive Action and Total Quality Management – The Involvement Gap

No formalized link between equality and Total Quality through involvement was found. At an individual level there was commitment to linking TQM to equal opportunities. Interviewees described KTAS as an equality organization at a general level, yet it was acknowledged that in traditional technical areas and in top management, an imbalance between the number of men and women remained. The interviewees felt that this may have had some impact on personal involvement in TQM. There is scope within KTAS to reduce the involvement gap and gain feedback from different groups within the organization for improving managerial efficiency. Redesigning TQM programmes by including the needs, aspirations and experiences of workers, stratified by gender, age and functional area, is likely to improve the goal of attaining consistency in quality.

Matra Ericsson Telecommunications (MET)

MET: Background Information

MET operates in the Public Telecommunications field, developing and supplying switches and exchanges. Until 1986, the present MET organization which supplied switches to France Telecom, was owned by the French Government. In 1986, the French Government offered all international organizations the opportunity to bid for a 100 percent share in the company. The requirements for the bid were that the bidding company had to team up with a French organization and guarantee a certain amount of exports from France. Ericsson won this contract in 1986/87, together with Matra, and formed the new company, Matra Ericsson Telecommunication (MET), France.

Matra is a large French industrial company, that together with Hachette, forms one of the largest publishing houses in the world. Together, the companies employ between 40 000 and 50 000 people and have sales of around ff50 billion. Ericsson is a multinational, Swedish-owned telecommunications company, which is active across Europe. The company is a major competitor of many of the private and newly-privatized telecommunications companies.

Today, MET in France operates in what has become one of the most highly digitalized telecommunication systems in the world: AXE.

Matra provide the Managing Director of MET and Ericsson provide the Chairman. Despite its dual national ownership, MET was described as having a "French" rather than "Swedish" culture. This has been encouraged by the number of expatriates working in MET being reduced from 40, two years ago, to the current number of 18. Rather than an overall culture, MET was described as having a number of subcultures.

When MET was first formed in 1987, the company employed

about 1900 people. After rationalization and the impact of technical change, the company now employs 1300 people. In the current recession there is little turnover of staff and of the 1300 people currently employed at MET, the average person has been with the organization for between 20 and 24 years. Only 200 people have been taken on in the last two years at MET and almost all of these have been recruited to the technical department. The company has an age pyramid of employees with almost no-one aged over 55 (mainly due to early retirement schemes being used during the retrenchment of the company), and most people are aged between 40 and 50 years.

Currently MET have a 15–16 percent share of the French switching market. This share was derived as the result of an agreement with France Telecom signed in 1987. It is a stable market agreement that currently cannot be altered. MET also exports from France and therefore is in a position where the company has to enforce its position in the Ericsson organization.

MET predicted a better market in the future with France Telecom. Expanding their market is important in order to maintain their current staffing levels. The company is extending its investment in training, both internally and externally. This training is mainly in the area of software development, where the company has a constant demand for people.

The Managing Director, Mr Lars Jarnryd described MET as:

"an optimistic and rich company looking for ways to expand."

Interviews within MET were conducted with the Managing Director, Directors; Managers and white-collar employees.

MET: Corporate Approach to Equal Opportunities and Positive Action

MET does not have a Corporate equal opportunities or positive action policy. During interviews with the Managing Director, the Personnel Director and a group of women managers from across the organization, it was the overall perception that the existing French legislation was sufficient in ensuring adherence to equality of opportunity within the organization. The fact that the company did not have an equal opportunity policy was largely regarded as being because equality within MET was followed as an unwritten rule.

In interviews with women middle management staff from MET, there was awareness of the disproportionate representation of women at the higher levels of management within the organization. Although representation at middle management was good, the women felt that in order to succeed within the company, they had to follow the same career route as the men. This often made it difficult to combine having a family and a career.

MET maintains records of the number of staff in different hierarchical positions within the organization, divided by gender, as well as salaries by hierarchical position and gender. These figures are far more comprehensive than the figures required by French legislation to be presented by the organization. The statistics are not used for equal opportunities monitoring purposes.

An illustrative example of employee data within MET is divided by the categories of engineers and higher management; middle management and blue-collar workers. The 1991 figures show that about *15 percent* of employees in engineering and higher management are women, just over *40 percent* of middle managers are women and just under *80 percent* of blue-collar workers are women.

Despite the fact that MET does not have a formal equality policy, initiatives exist within the company that reflect the values of equality.

Provisions for part-time working exist within MET. It is also possible for both men and women to take career breaks. However, it was generally agreed upon by the women interviewees that taking a career break would severely slow down the progression of an individual's career.

Due to the transference within MET to the new manufacturing technology, a large number of staff at this level has had to be shed, many of them women. The labour cost entailed within production used to be 50 percent of the entire product cost, today it is 15 percent. With the introduction of further new technology this figure could drop still further. Attempts have been made within MET to cross-train staff from the old to the new technologies wherever possible. However, the highest demand for cross-training is in the area of software engineering and only 10–15 percent of redundant employees have succeeded in being cross-trained to this area, due in large part to the background skills required for this work.

MET: Positive Action/Equal Opportunities – A Summary

MET do not have a policy on positive action or equal opportunities. The general view gained from the interviews was that the company had a culture that reflected equality and that the existing French legislation was sufficient to ensure inequality did not arise.

However, interviewees were aware of the gender imbalance present in the upper levels of management. It was also felt that a fairly strict career path had to be followed by both men and women in order to progress within the company. This career path did not allow to a great extent for the needs of diverse groups within the organization.

MET: Corporate Approach to Total Quality Management

Achieving Total Quality has become a strategic factor within MET, helping to enable them to realize their strategic aims.

The pursuit of Total Quality follows MET's achievement of ISO 9000 certification.

The MET approach to TQM contains four core values, communicated to employees with the aid of posters and through ongoing training courses (Figure 5.2).

problem prevention	listening to customers
zero defects	"best cost" (not necessarily the highest or lowest cost)

Figure 5.2   Quality Values at MET

The Director for Quality within MET has overall responsibility for the implementation of Total Quality within the organization. The quality group also includes Directors from other functions with individuals responsible for quality reporting to them (Figure 5.3).

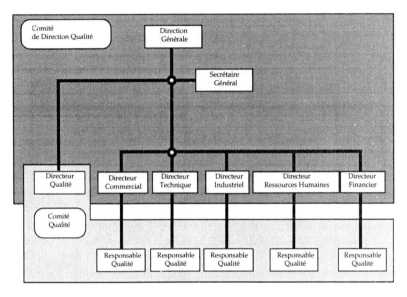

Figure 5.3   Organization of Total Quality at MET

Total Quality is being implemented within MET in stages. The first area to adopt Quality Management was the production area. MET have been working to harmonize quality throughout the company for the past year and a half. This is being achieved through distribution of the Quality Manual, complemented by posters displaying the four values of quality and training courses.

Tools for Quality Improvement

(1) Project Teams   At the present time, the aims of quality are being followed within the already existent structures of project teams within the company. The project teams each have a quality plan, the objectives of which have been decided by top management. These are not specifically quality teams as

such, but project teams that are aware of quality issues. Quality improvement teams are planned to be set up at a later stage.

(2) Suggestion Scheme At present, no formalized mechanism exists for suggestions to be made by employees on improving the work process. It is planned that once a clear view of what quality means within the organization has been understood generally, the mechanisms for implementing suggestion schemes will be set in place.

(3) Training for TQM Training courses, set up to enhance the communication of the quality message, began within MET in September 1992. In its first stage, training was given to 100 of the highest level managers (starting with the Board of Directors). The next phase plans to provide training for 300 managers and employees.

MET: The Future Challenges of Total Quality

MET have a number of aims to be achieved in the pursuit of TQM within the organization. Within the statement of these aims the responsibilities of the Quality manager and committee are also stipulated. These aims, as detailed below have been communicated to each member of the company through the Quality Manual.

- quality projects for approval by the Quality Committee should be prepared;
- it should be ensured that the Manual reaches each employee within MET;
- the implementation of quality should be monitored by the Quality Committee;
- the Quality Manager should liaise with other departments in order to define objectives for improving quality;
- the Quality Manager should liaise with independent Quality bodies;
- the Quality Manager has responsibility for contact with MET's clients to answer their questions on quality issues;
- the Quality Manager has responsibility for ensuring that MET's clients understand that the products and services produced at MET are different from other company's products

and services as they have been produced to the company's standards of quality.

It was envisaged that certain barriers exist, that need to be overcome in order to fully implement quality within the company. The barriers are perceived to arise largely from the difficulty that some employees within the company have with the acceptance of quality as a management philosophy. For some employees, Total Quality Management is regarded simply as another management phase. The Quality Director stated:

> "It's a tough problem, my approach is to show people quality is not a mode and that quality is a help for everybody and a necessity for the life of the company and for their job."

MET: Total Quality Management – A Summary

The pursuit of TQM is claimed by the Vice President and Director General of MET as being of strategic importance to the future competitiveness of the company. Having achieved ISO 9000 certification for the industrial area, MET is now working towards certification for the whole company and implementing the wider values and objectives of their quality policy. This is being achieved in stages through a quality manual and quality training.

One of the greatest challenges currently facing MET in their implementation of TQM, is overcoming the barriers the different organizational subcultures pose to achieving a common understanding and commitment to the quality values and objectives.

MET: Positive Action and Total Quality Management – The Involvement Gap

In its pursuit of TQ, the importance of involvement has been acknowledged within MET. However, explicit strategies by which such involvement can be attained has not been made. While the interviewees made it clear that MET operated as an equal opportunities company, without a policy which stated this explicitly, it was difficult to ensure that the needs and aspirations of diverse groups were addressed adequately. This, together with the problem of achieving universal understanding of the values and objectives of TQ within MET could be redressed through an integrated TQM and positive action initiative.

The Greek Telecommunications Company (OTE)

OTE: Background Information

OTE was established as a State monopoly in 1949. Its present work force consists of around 27 000 employees. Currently, the Greek Government is considering plans to privatize 35 percent of OTE. Such moves towards privatization would also include a change from public to private management. The move comes at a time of increased deregulation and competition in the telecommunications industry across Europe.

Interviews were carried out with representatives from the company and Union within OTE (the Greek Telecommunications Workers Federation, OME OTE).

It should be noted that the improvements and initiatives described below that have occurred within OTE on the issue of equal opportunities has had a positive influential effect within other industries in Greece such as rail and electricity.

OTE: Corporate Approach to Equal Opportunities and Positive Action

Telecommunications in Greece was traditionally a sector characterized by labour segregation. Until 1979 separate job categories existed for men and women. Also, until this time, women were not permitted to enter the technical or administrative fields.

Moves to abolish job segregation occurred within OTE following the implementation of equality laws in Greece in 1975. As a result of such changes in the State legislation, companies also began to change their constitutions as regards women in the context of recruitment, training and promotion. In 1979, women in OTE were first allowed to enter administrative roles, and in 1985, women began to enter jobs in the technical field. In 1983, after considerable Union action, the administrative and telephone operator job categories were merged, enabling women to have better access to career progression and enabling moves towards equal pay for men and women within the job category. Thus, in 1983, separate job categories for women were abolished within OTE and the company changed its constitution in the same year to state that it was an equal opportunities employer.

In terms of the aims of the policy, since the change in State legislation in 1975, significant changes have occurred within OTE with the aim of redressing organizational inequalities. The overall aims of OTE's equal opportunities policy include: abolishing job segregation, promotion of women into decision-making roles, abolishing unequal pay.

Regarding the employee profile, women constitute a statistically small proportion of employees within OTE. They are concentrated in the lower levels of the organization, predominantly in blue-collar level jobs. Few women are represented in middle management with no women represented at the top levels of the organization.

Positive Action and Equal Opportunity Initiatives

In order to work towards achieving the aims of equal opportunities within OTE, a committee consisting of Trade Unions, Management, Personnel and a representative from the Ministry of Labour has been established that has responsibility for equal opportunities.

(1) Monitoring   The committee's work on equal opportunities has made many achievements since its formation in 1985. One of the first initiatives undertaken by the committee was the launch of a positive action programme in 1985. Agreement for this programme was achieved through collective bargaining. The Programme aimed to examine the position of women within the organization as well as to make an analysis of the company's policies as regards recruitment, promotion, training and health and safety. Following the results of the audit, it was the aim that concrete proposals could be made to work towards improving the position of women within the company. It was claimed that the greatest benefit of this study was that statistical information

in these areas could now be gathered to provide a clear picture of the organization.

A number of findings from the Positive Action audit emerged. Firstly it was found that women constitute a small proportion of OTE employees primarily concentrated in the lower levels of the company. Also, there are no women in top management positions within the organization. Secondly, the number of men and women educated to University level was almost equal, however, University educated women had not progressed to the equivalent levels that the men had reached. Finally, women were not motivated to stay within the company for a large number of years.

Following the results of the audit, the committee lobbied for the appointment of an equal opportunities officer to enable follow up action to be taken. To date, such an appointment has not been agreed. However, the committee continues to make considerable improvements in its work in this area. Currently, women also now have a presence within the management of OTE.

(2) Networking   Through the Union, action has been taken to raise women's awareness within OTE. This has been achieved through seminars and information leaflets. A network of women in telecommunications has also been established. Its first meeting was on 14 June 1990.

(3) Flexi-Work Organization   Although opportunities for part-time work within OTE exist, these are generally not made use of as the wages are regarded as being too low to make such flexi-working worthwhile. For this reason, to date, women's organizations have, in general opposed part-time working. Tele-working or home-working has not yet been introduced within OTE.

(4) Training   Although no specific training to raise awareness of the issues of equal opportunities has taken place within OTE, training to enable women to enter the administrative fields took place in 1983. This occurred as a result of the merging of the different job categories and roles.

The merging of the job categories has also helped the retraining of women on new technology to take place. To date, no redundancies have occurred due to the introduction of new technology. All employees have received retraining in the new skills required. However, the threat of new technology to jobs is predicted to increase in the future.

With reference to the progress that has been made within OTE as regards equality of opportunity for women, an interviewee expressed the feeling that:

> "Things were so bad, so many things had to change, it was not easy to bring this change. If we look back ten years or so, we can see that many things have changed."

OTE: Positive Action and Equal Opportunities: The Future

Despite the changes and improvements that have taken place within OTE as regards equal opportunities, there is the feeling within the organization that many more improvements remain to be made. As one interviewee pointed out:

> "In theory we have equality, but what about the previous discrimination?"

It was felt in particular, that although the initiatives taken to date have benefited women entering the company, more needed to be done towards developing women already employed within OTE.

Specific points of improvement were highlighted in the interviews, namely, to increase the number of women in decision-making roles, a suggested increase in training for women, specifically in the area of new technology and, to develop positive action to increase the number of women working in areas involving new technology.

OTE: Positive Action and Equal Opportunities: Barriers to Future Policy Aims

Certain barriers were identified by interviewees to the achievement of further improvements to equal opportunities in the future. These were as follows:

- education of women predominantly in the Classics, rather than technological fields;
- lack of general support and consciousness within the Union and company for equal opportunity issues, however, there

was the perception that the younger women within the company were now more motivated to progress their careers;
* current economic and political climate: During the current period of uncertainty concerning the issue of privatization, it was felt that equal opportunity issues have had to take second place. It was suggested that:

> "If the situation was different, many proposals of the committee would be accepted. But now it is difficult."

* social, cultural and political barriers: The double burden placed on women in Greek society of caring for the family, children and the elderly, mean that developing a career can be difficult. In addition, with only 14 women out of 300 in Parliament, the lack of role models and women in political decision-making roles was also seen as a barrier within OTE, a company highly influenced by politics.

OTE: Positive Action/Equal Opportunities – A Summary

Significant moves have been made within OTE to improve the quantity and quality of women's work. This has been signified by the abolition of job segregation for men and women and the increasing number of women currently entering the company in all areas, including the technical fields. Due to the mechanisms set in place by the positive action study, data on the position of women in OTE can now easily be collected.

The main challenges currently facing OTE are twofold. Firstly there arises the question of how to implement strategies and initiatives that further enable women to progress their careers within the company. Secondly, there is the problem of how to maintain commitment to and impetus of the objectives of positive action in an increasingly challenging and uncertain organizational and market environment.

OTE: Corporate Approach to Total Quality

Although some quality initiatives are being taken within OTE, for example within the Customer Relations Department, widespread

Total Quality Management (TQM) has not yet been implemented. However, Quality Management as a philosophy is currently being considered. What follows is an account of the process followed so far towards making the decision to implement Total Quality and an insight into the problems that the company believe they will face on the road to implementation.

The first moves towards Quality Management started in 1982 when, with the assistance of the Welsh Region of British Telecom, a feasibility study was carried out. Impetus for this move came from the widespread maintenance problems that the company was experiencing at that time. A survey of users was conducted in order to try and find key areas where quality needed to be improved.

The next action towards Quality Management did not occur until nearly ten years later when, in 1991, a group of nine people from the department responsible for Structural and Operational Systems were commissioned by the top Administration of OTE to investigate the feasibility of implementing Total Quality. The project was commissioned due to the widespread problem the company was experiencing with service to its users, both individuals and other organizations. This project spanned six months. The results of this project were presented to the Administration in 1992. The team, now disbanded, await the Administration's response.

Two main conclusions arose from the project. Firstly, there is an urgent need to improve the quality of the technical aspects of the organization, such as the switching equipment. Secondly, a need exists to improve the quality of the existing highly bureaucratic service to customers, including improvement of information to customers via the various services in existence. The methods through which these recommendations could be implemented fell into two broad categories: Technological investment and human resource management.

It was the view of the feasibility study group that the first recommendation could be carried out swiftly through investment in new technology and the benefits of this could be reaped in the short term.

The group predicted that the implementation of Quality Management would be made exceedingly difficult due to the "human factor" involved.

The quality group proposed to the administration that Total Quality Management should be implemented through use of management by objective techniques. Objectives, although largely set by top management, would ensure that consultation was made with all levels of staff before being set, to ensure their endorsement by all levels of staff. This method was recommended, it was stated, to try and overcome a present problem of lack of accountability within OTE.

Under the issue of human resource management, two main barriers to successful implementation of Total Quality Management were envisaged: a lack of commitment and participation given by top management in the Administration, and also the problem of convincing general employees that:

"they are the stones on which the success of the company rests."

The quality group stated that people were always opposed to change and that despite the benefits, it was often difficult to persuade people to change. Although no proposals were put forward by the group for overcoming the first and what was highlighted as the largest barrier, suggestions were made as to how involvement from employees could be sought. These included ensuring quality new recruits, continuous on the job training, increased salaries (to increase motivation), and increased job satisfaction through improving the respect for the individual at all levels.

The benefits of implementing Total Quality were seen by the team as from both the customer's and company's view.

From the customer's viewpoint, it was felt that two key benefits from the implementation of TQM would be realized: better quality in all services and faster solution to users problems.

From OTE's viewpoint, it was felt that the benefits to be gleaned from implementing TQM would include greater prestige for the company in society, and the direct benefits resulting from increased use of services.

As a final point, it should be noted that the team strongly believed in the benefits of Total Quality and hoped that implementation would follow. As one interviewee firmly stated:

"I want quality to go ahead. Things can't go on like this."

OTE: Positive Action and Total Quality Management: The Involvement Gap

OTE acknowledged the importance of employee involvement in achieving TQM. However, the role of positive action programmes in achieving such involvement was not explicitly made. A large proportion of women did not stay long-term within the company, many women leave the company after only a few years as it becomes difficult for them to combine a career and family. This suggests that women may not have a feeling of involvement with the organization.

The current period within OTE is characterized by more women entering the company in technical fields. Women's career aspirations are visibly rising. This is taking place in an environment of increased competitive challenges for OTE which may be moving towards the implementation of TQM. This seems an appropriate time for OTE to increase the level of involvement women have with the organization in order to achieve the strategic goals of corporate efficiency. Organizations inside and outside Greece can learn from the determination and progress that has been made within OTE as regards positive action. In turn, OTE can also benefit from the experiences of other European telecommunication organizations, particularly with respect to integrating positive action into the TQ process, as opposed to implementing the two policies separately.

Italtel

Italtel: Background Information

Italtel is Italy's largest telecommunications equipment manufacturer. In 1991, consolidated sales totalled 2760.2 billion lire, with over half of this produced from the sales of public switching. Italtel has, in the last ten years, been undergoing a change process from employing electro-mechanical to electrical technology. During this period, Italtel's workforce has also been reduced from around 30 000 employees to employing just under

16 000 employees today. The uncertain environment for Italtel continues as the company currently addresses the issues of joint partnership strategy and the Government consider proposals for deregulation of the Industry. Given the strategic nature of the industry, it is unlikely that it will be totally deregulated. However, the threat of continued job losses within the company from the possible changes continues. The jobs that are most at risk are in the area of blue collar workers, around 80 percent of whom are women. At this stage, however, it is difficult to determine whether job cuts will arise from deregulation or technological changes.

The management philosophy at Italtel has changed substantially with the introduction of Total Quality Management. The introduction has also brought structural changes. Prior to TQM, the organization had a vertical structure. This has now changed to a matrix structure helping the organization to move towards having a holistic approach in its operations.

Interviews at Italtel were carried out with representatives from Human Resource Management, Quality Management, the Unions, UILM; FIM and CGIL and operatives.

Italtel: Corporate Approach to Positive Action and Equal Opportunities

Moves towards equal opportunities within Italtel first developed in 1986. Such moves were initiated by the Unions during 1981, at a time of severe job cuts within the organization. The job cuts came, in part due to the transition from electro-mechanical to electrical technology. The job cuts brought with them a change in the profile and location of Italtel's workforce. Previously, about 70 percent of Italtel's workforce were blue collar. Today, about 80 percent of the staff are white-collar workers. Of the remaining blue collar workers, about 80 percent are women. The change in technology was accompanied by a change strategy of gradually moving all manufacturing operations to the south of Italy. This move predominantly affected the women employees who were concentrated in the manufacturing positions within the company.

The Unions (UILM, FIM & CGIL) felt that women were becoming penalized during the period when employees were being retrained in the new technical skills needed in manufacturing.

More men than women were being retrained, meaning that whilst the men moved up in the organization, women became stagnated at the lower levels. There was the perception that discrimination also existed in the way that the retraining was presented to women. It was presented as being highly technical and the mobility factor, that the women would have to move to the south of Italy (as manufacturing was being transferred to L'Aquila, Palermo, Santa Maria Capua Vetere and Terni) was presented as a disadvantage for the women taking up retraining. The Unions brought this problem to the attention of management. Subsequently, in 1985, an agreement between the management and Unions was signed agreeing to training specifically for women.

A move towards equal opportunities was also stimulated at this time by Maria Belisario, the then Chief Executive Officer of Italtel, who was also a member of the State Equal Opportunities Group.

Positive action programmes within Italtel aim to ensure equality of opportunity for women in recruitment, promotion and training. More specifically, current aims focus on improving maternity leave and opportunities for women to return to work following childbirth as well as ensuring job segregation amongst men and women is abolished.

Whilst the distribution of men and women at middle management level is fairly equal within Italtel, few women can be found in top management positions. Women are heavily concentrated in the blue collar worker positions at the level of production. Moves to redress the imbalance of women within the more technical field of work have resulted in an increase in the percentage of women within Research and Development from 0 percent in 1981 to 23 percent in 1993.

Positive Action and Equal Opportunity Initiatives

(1) Monitoring   A Commission has been set up within Italtel consisting of Union representatives, management, and external researchers and experts to assist in the process of equal opportunities and positive action. A task of this group was also to gain a picture of the overall position of women within Italtel. A report resulted from this research and negotiations followed on how the position of women in Italtel could be improved. Agreement was

reached that action should be taken within the organization to redress the inequalities present. Five agreements were made including proposals for different types of work organization that would allow room for women's professional growth. An example of an initiative resulting from these agreements was that training was established to help women develop inter-functional skills. It was stated that:

> "By gaining more skills and knowing how the entire process works, you can help women's position in the workforce."

In addition to the overall task force, separate "Observatory" (or monitoring) groups in different Divisions within Italtel have been established to monitor the progress of these initiatives. The Milan Observatory group is made up of 15 members, 9 from the Trade Union and 6 from the Company. Company members are from Director level, one of whom is a woman. The Observatories currently have a formalized yearly plan, set out from corporate level, detailing initiatives to be taken in the area of positive action. These include initiatives in the areas of: recruitment and selection, maternity leave and returners and work segregation.

(2) Networking   The Unions have also taken specific action to raise awareness within Italtel of equal opportunities and positive action through information leaflets and seminars. Women are being encouraged to apply for what have been traditionally considered as "male jobs".

(3) Flexi-Work Organization   Provision exists within Italtel for both men and women to work part-time and flexi-work hours.

(4) Training   The first positive action initiatives within Italtel concerned the retraining of women in the new technology. However, this first agreement restricted the training to women at a certain level only. A subsequent agreement succeeded in extending this training to women at other levels.

(5) Research   Italtel also conducted research in the area of positive action for women within the European telecommunications manufacturing sector in 1993. The Project, funded by the European Commission, included companies from France, USA, Spain, Sweden, UK and Germany. The study gathered information on the different approaches taken within the organizations of these countries to positive action. The aim of

the project was to establish common indicators of the position of women within different telecommunication organizations, to verify the different influences of the corporate policies and to establish a system of benchmarking with European and worldwide partners.

Italtel: Positive Action and Equal Opportunities: The Future

Through the findings of the European Research project, and the continuation of development towards the goals stated in Italtel's yearly positive action and equal opportunity plan, the company wishes to further improve the position and professional scope of women within the organization, who make up around 60 percent of the workforce.

Through interviews, two elements were highlighted as specific improvements that needed to be made in equal opportunities within Italtel. Firstly, it was felt important to increase awareness and commitment to the goals of positive action and equal opportunities. A second area for improvement involved the need to increase retraining of women, in particular into traditional male areas of work.

In terms of retraining women, work in this area continues within Italtel. The importance of retraining women has been highlighted during the present recession as redundancies continue to be necessary. Although it is possible for much of this wastage to go in the form of early retirement, the Unions are concerned that many of the redundancies are made at the lowest levels of the organization, predominantly made up of women. Women at this level, without professional or technical training would find it the most difficult to find alternative employment. The proposal from the Union is that women should be retrained and retraining into traditional male jobs should be considered. To this end, reducing the male bias in internal job advertisements and in internal interviews has already been achieved.

Italtel: Positive Action and Equal Opportunities: Barriers to Future Policy Aims

Evidence was shown during interviews that the level of awareness within the company of the importance and relevance of positive action has risen. However, concern was expressed by interviewees that the positive action projects were at times regarded by employees as pilot projects, rather than part of a longer-term strategy. The perception of interviewees was that commitment to positive action from the majority of management and some men in the Union was lower than desired. These interviewees felt that further work was required to raise commitment throughout Italtel to positive action.

Italtel: Positive Action/Equal Opportunities – A Summary

In 1981, a woman, Maria Belisario, became Chief Executive of Italtel and since 1986, when positive action initiatives were first developed within Italtel, considerable development has been made within the company towards achieving the goals of equal opportunities. With a strong input from the Unions (UILM, FIM, CGIL), Italtel has succeeded in retraining women in new technical and inter-functional skills in order to encourage development of their careers. Women have also been encouraged through awareness-raising initiatives and networking to apply for traditionally male jobs. In order to gain a greater understanding of the positive action initiatives being undertaken within other telecommunications organizations outside Italy, Italtel have also undertaken their own, EC-funded research in this area. However, interviewees felt that awareness and commitment to the goals of positive action needed to be raised further throughout the organization. The company is also still working towards increasing the retraining of women, in particular into traditionally male areas of work.

Italtel: Corporate Approach to Total Quality Management

Having achieved ISO 9000 certification, Italtel have expanded their pursuit of quality towards the achievement of Total Quality Management (TQM). The introduction of TQM has substantially changed the management philosophy within the company. For example, prior to TQM, Italtel was vertically arranged and activities were oriented only towards the final client, with little evidence of "team spirit" within the company. Italtel now has a matrix structure. The emphasis within the company is now on having a holistic approach through interfunctionality. In addition, focus has expanded and the client base is now regarded as including not only the final customer, but also other clients within the firm.

Italtel has a competitive approach to its strategic vision of quality. The quality strategy is made up of three different dimensions including product, service, and human relations.

Italtel also has five basic quality values, including:

- the customer comes first;
- all work is part of a process;
- quality improvement is continuous;
- prevention is achieved through planning;
- quality happens through people.

These principles and values form the basics to Italtel's current work on quality.

The final principle and value is a new dimension in quality for Italtel and they stated that it is regarded as the fundamental underpinning for success of their policy. Italtel also stated that this final element directly affects women in Italtel who make up around 60 percent of the workforce.

Italtel have taken a systemic approach to quality used in conjunction with a defined set of priorities. Without systematic application of the most advanced quality methodologies, Italtel stated that they believed results cannot be achieved.

Business Unit Systems Radio: A Case-Study Example

Introduction of Total Quality Management techniques within manufacturing are shown clearly within the case example of the Systems Radio business unit within Italtel.

(1) Organization   Three years ago, Italtel in the area of production were concerned with quantity but not with quality. Today, quantity quotas are in operation that work alongside three standards of quality for employees to work towards. A reward system is attached to the different levels of quality achievement.

For example, if production workers achieve the first standard of quality, they would receive an additional payment in their monthly salary. This process was first introduced in order to help Italtel to work towards achieving ISO 9000 certification.

Within this business unit of 300 people, ten groups exist, each with a leader. The balance in the number of men and women leading groups within this unit is equal. Leaders are appointed by management within the business unit.

(2) Work Organization The organization of work within this unit has been changed. Previously, the product would be assembled by a number of individual tasks carried out by individuals responsible for one task each. The testing of the quality of this product was carried out in a different department. Today, the same group assembles and tests the product. In addition, job rotation has been introduced into the unit in order to develop workers to be more holistic and accountable in their approach.

(3) Training Training was given to individuals so that they were capable of carrying out more than one task. Within this training, the importance of the supplier customer relationship is stressed. The customer, it is explained, is not the enemy, but someone who can help them in their job.

(4) Involvement Once the quality and quantity targets have been set, the workers are asked to agree to these targets and "sign" up to them. Each week, discussion of progress towards quality achievements are discussed within the group, together with a member from the quality department. It is through these meetings for example, that suggestions for quality improvement would be made.

In general, it is reported that people are now achieving the highest level of quality. Notices of different groups' achievements towards achieving the set quality levels are displayed regularly each week. Within the unit, about fifteen people work part-time. It is ensured that team meetings, announcements and training are always arranged for periods when the part-time employees are at work.

(5) Overcoming Problems Some problems were experienced with convincing each worker of the benefits of job rotation and quality. Some people were unwilling to learn another task and felt that they were the only ones who could carry out that particular

task. In order to get over this problem, intense communication took place. This communication came from the very top level of management. Workers were shown that managers had time for them in order to resolve the problem.

(6) Heightening Customer Awareness and Involvement The customer (The Italian State Holding Company, SIP) regularly visits the production unit. A method of certification has also been established by Italtel with their customer (SIP) of standards and quality. This is a separate customer agreement to that used within ISO 9000. SIP are now concerned with how production is carried out and visits the company 6 times a year for two or three days at a time. It is reported that this practice has changed the attitude of the worker. Traditionally the customer has always been seen as the responsibility of management. If the customer goes elsewhere, that was seen as the responsibility and fault of management. With the introduction of this practice, the workers realized the customer was interested in what they were doing and how responsible they were for the success of the company.

Organization for TQM

Responsibility for ensuring the mechanism for achieving quality is in place within Italtel is held at five points within the organization. The actors in this process include:

- Quality Councils, made up of top management;
- Quality Specialists, made up of middle managers;
- Quality Champions, made up of leaders in the quality field located in training session;
- Personnel, at various levels in the organization;
- Unions.

Quality Measures

Quality at the level of the product is measured specifically in terms of defect reduction and productivity improvement. Measurement is also carried out in terms of the achievement of stated customer oriented goals.

Tools for Quality Improvement

It was stated at Italtel that the success of implementing TQM depends on imparting the following skills to all employees: business focus, market focus, and human development focus. Italtel believes that, in order to achieve a quantum leap towards TQM, the human resource development process demands a change in attitudes; awareness; structures and performance.

(1) The Quality Leadership Programme   The Quality Leadership concept aims to reflect the acknowledged changes that need to take place within the field of human resource development in order to achieve Total Quality. The Quality leadership concept illustrates to members of Italtel what it means to be a good quality manager or employee. The concept involves the following three central assumptions that need to be followed in pursuit of Total Quality:

(i)   to lead the quality process with facts and not only words: *there is a strong reporting mechanism within Italtel for quality which is measured regularly. The tool, management by data, is heavily used.*
(ii) to lead the company to quality improvement through the systematic deployment application: *quality deployment is used as the basic way of improvement within Italtel.*
(iii) to assign, communicate, support and supervise the achievement of customer-oriented goals: *this aim requires a lot of attention to communication, support and motivation with collaborators in order to ensure its achievement.*

To implement quality in offices (not just manufacturing) a number of tools are used within Italtel. The use of these tools and the implications they have for the structural organization of the company are discussed regularly in consultation with the Unions within Italtel.

(2) Quality System Tools   The quality system tool is implemented through use of ISO 9000 techniques. That is, the procedures of ISO 9000 are used to make people aware of the demands of quality. Italtel have now reached the stage where each Head of Function in the organization is aware of their duties in relation to quality.

(3) Process Analysis Tools   Currently each process of the company is being worked through to see where improvements can be made. For example, Research and Development (R&D) is currently being examined. One function of R&D covers the process of whether a component can be authorized for use in manufacturing. The lead time on this process has been improved to shorten it from 19 to 3 weeks. In order to achieve this improvement, project teams were established that spanned across the relevant functions involved with the authorization process.

(4) Quality Improvement Teams   Quality improvement teams are established from islands of workers taken from throughout Italtel. Each island consists of between 25 and 30 workers and to date, at least 400 islands of workers have been formed. Through these islands, workers are encouraged to lead the organization to quality through the systematic deployment approach and to assign, communicate, support and supervise the customer oriented goals of Italtel.

Leaders of the groups are chosen according to the hierarchical levels involved within the process being addressed. For example, if the project covers different functionalities, a manager and probably a high manager will be chosen as leader. If the process is contained within one function, a member of staff (non managerial) may be chosen. If the process is on a manufacturing level, a worker may be chosen to lead the group.

Of the leaders currently in place (process owners), 90 percent are men and only 10 percent are women. This reflects the low number of women represented at the higher level of the hierarchy.

(5) TQM Specialists   Within Italtel, a group of four TQM specialists are employed, all of whom are women. These specialists have been recruited from Universities where they have been conducting theses in Quality Management. The Quality Director indicated that the majority of theses students in the field in Italy today are women.

(6) Total Quality Management and Involvement   Italtel have taken two major steps towards improving the involvement level of employees within the company. The first of these concerns the level of training for employees.

(7) Training for TQM   It was highlighted within the organization, that prior to 1989, that on average, only a few hours per

year were given to employees for education and training. To illustrate the investment Italtel believe they are making in their staff, last year, on average, five days were given per employee for training during the year. In addition, education and training programmes are continuing for managers each year in the area of quality.

(8) TQM Reward System Within the managerial hierarchical levels of the company, Management by Objectives (MBO) techniques are employed to gain increased involvement from employees. In 1992, 30–40 percent of objectives were related to quality.

In the area of production, three levels of quality achievement have been set (these levels have been set by top management). Monetary rewards are given to workers depending on which level of quality they achieve in production. The rewards increase with the higher levels of quality standards.

Customer involvement in the production process has also been increased through the use of satisfaction surveys. As was illustrated in the case-study example of the System Radio business unit, customers are also invited to see the production process in action at regular intervals during the year, achieving increase levels in both customer and employee involvement.

Italtel: The Future Challenges of Total Quality Management

Italtel identified the following three major strengths in their pursuit of Total Quality Management to date:

- achievement of commitment, perseverance and determination by top management to the philosophy of Total Quality Management;
- achievement of clearly stated Total Quality objectives;
- achievement of the use of advanced methodologies and tools in pursuit of quality, including customer perception, people satisfaction and ISO 9000.

Such achievements have meant that major quality improvements have been made within Italtel, for example, the number of defects in production across the company has been reduced by 75 percent.

In continuing to work towards the stated goals of TQM, Italtel have realized the areas of weakness in the approach taken so far. Future action aims to overcome these weaknesses in the following ways:

weakness: Lack of quality leadership in some managers.
overcome by: Training for managers.
weakness: Deployment process is not yet expanded to lower levels of the hierarchy. overcome by: Deployment process being developed further down the organization through the "catchbowl process". This is a process whereby "bottom-up" proposals (derived from the lower levels of the organization hierarchy) are compared to "top-down" proposals (derived from the upper levels of the organization hierarchy). The visions of the same problem and the different approaches to the same goal are compared. The ideas are then merged and a decision for action is taken. This technique is being introduced in 1993/94.
weakness: A tendency by employees to consider quality as something additional to their everyday work and not as a way of working.
overcome by: Workshops, communications and commitment to TQM from the top.
weakness: Cultural reluctance within the company to shift towards interfunctionality.
overcome by: Bringing the worker and customer closer together and raising awareness of the importance of TQM to organizational competitiveness and survival.

Italtel: Total Quality Management – A Summary

The introduction of TQM within Italtel has brought with it many changes and benefits for the company. Italtel now has a matrix organizational structure and the number of defects in products has dramatically fallen. Interfunctionality has increased and employees are now more client-conscious. Such improvements have been achieved in part through use of quality improvement tools such as suggestion schemes, a reward system and in part by Italtel's acknowledgement of the importance of employee involvement. Through the third quality principle, "quality through people" Italtel believe the objectives of positive action can help the company achieve full involvement from employees.

Italtel: Positive Action and Total Quality Management – The Involvement Gap

Italtel perceive a strong connection between the pursuit of the goals of Total Quality and those of equal opportunities and positive action. It is believed that this connection is being made through the third principle of Total Quality within Italtel, that of "quality through people".

> "A Quality policy exists and one of the most important values of this policy is related to Human Resources."

The process analysis techniques used in pursuit of Total Quality within the company are gender neutral. The processes have deliberately been related to skills in an attempt to try and move the company away from its traditional "macho" or male image and bias.

> "If a woman has talent, through TQM is the most rapid way of progressing. Before, there were a number of cultural assumptions that were blocking women's progress. If someone can master TQM techniques, they are successful."

Italtel stated that it is currently considering following the European Foundation for Quality Management(EFQM) approach to employee or "people" involvement.

Further development of this concept, that of the link between the objectives of positive action and TQ, may help Italtel in overcoming some of their stated present TQ weaknesses. Areas of improvement may include increased involvement of employees at the lower levels of the organization, encouraging interfunctionality and improving commitment to the goals of TQ.

Ericsson Limited (UK) (ETL)

ETL: Background Information

Ericsson is a multinational, Swedish-owned telecommunications company, which is active across Europe and the world. The company is a major supplier to many of the private and newly-privatized telecommunications companies.

ETL is situated within a market that is becoming increasingly open and competitive due to deregulation and the implementation of the European Single Market offering greater opportunities to the company. As ETL has streamlined its business, some redundancies have been necessary in peripheral areas. However, recruitment in core technical areas continue. Competitive challenges have led to an organizational restructure. The potential opportunities in the increasingly open market place has also added increased urgency to achieving the benefits brought by comprehensive implementation of Total Quality Management within the company.

Seven interviews within ETL were carried out with management and staff from the Quality, and Personnel departments, across two divisions. Whilst some factual information is included in the results below, due to the small sample of interviews carried out within ETL, the opinions and perceptions of interviewees should not be taken as representative of the company as a whole.

ETL: Corporate Approach to Equal Opportunities and Positive Action

ETL has no positive action programme, however, whilst discussion concerning the implementation of an equal opportunities policy within ETL has existed for some time, actual implementation took place in 1993, following about nine months of preparation. The equal opportunity policy has been implemented by ETL's Personnel Working Party which includes representatives from each of the organization's Divisions. This group assesses personnel policies that affect all Divisions in order to maintain consistency in their approaches. Whilst interviews revealed the strong influence that exists within ETL from Ericsson in Sweden, impetus for implementing the equal opportunity policy did not derive from Sweden. However, it should be noted that currently, initiatives to promote the number of women in management in Ericsson, Sweden are underway.

It is the aim within ETL that the equal opportunities policy should be implemented within the organization in stages in order to communicate its objectives to staff. It is planned to introduce this primarily through examples of good working practices.

The ETL equal opportunity policy aims to:

> "work towards offering equality for all, across the entire spectrum of employment, regardless of an individuals: sex, age, race, colour, religion, ethnic or national origin, union membership, marital status or disability" (Ericsson Ltd (UK) Equal Opportunities Policy and Good Working Practices, No. 1551–FEAG 102/07).

Within ETL, interviewees felt that a proportional representation of both men and women existed at middle management level, whilst top managers were perceived as being predominantly male. There was the suggestion that the technical and engineering cultural nature of the company was, in part, an explanation of this imbalance. That is, that women had not traditionally gained technical qualifications. This explanation was reflected in the number of women that were grouped within the administrative roles and the Personnel Function as opposed to the predominance of men within the engineering, installation and sales functions.

With the recent introduction of an equal opportunities policy within ETL, no equal opportunity initiatives had been set in place. However, several working parties were found already in operation that reflect the values of equal opportunities. This supported the general view of the interviewees that the policy was formalizing current good practice.

ETL operates a flexi-time policy that both men and women participate in. Some jobs also operate on a part-time contract basis. Recently, a separate sheet has been included with job application forms designed to collect data reflecting good equal opportunity and personnel working practices. A new personnel computer system is also being introduced to facilitate the gathering of such data.

ETL: Positive Action and Equal Opportunities: The Future

Interviews showed that action would be taken within ETL to improve equal opportunities within the areas of training, development and recruitment. (in the recruitment area this means instilling a non-discriminatory philosophy within managers when they are recruiting).

Such action, it was stated, would take place primarily through leading by good example.

ETL: Positive Action and Equal Opportunities: Barriers to Future Policy Aims

Whilst it should be stressed that from the interviews, it was the general feeling amongst the interviewees that no fundamental barriers to implementing equal opportunities existed, two interviewees felt that some difficulties may arise identifying problems in transforming the organizational culture in the ways in which the policy implies, problems arising from the traditional view of the role of women held in society, and, finally, problems in promoting women in technical areas due to the current overall lack of potential for recruitment.

ETL: Positive Action/Equal Opportunities – A Summary

An equal opportunities policy has only recently been introduced to ETL. However, working practices that reflect equality of opportunity have been in place within ETL for some time, such as the operation of flexi-work hours. A policy has been introduced in order to ensure further development towards equal opportunities is achieved, specifically in the areas of recruitment, development and training.

ETL: Corporate Approach to Quality Management

Total Quality (TQ) is distinguished in ETL from Total Quality Management (TQM). TQ has been more concerned with conformance to requirements principally through the achievement of ISO 9000. Underpinning this is "quality" which is seen corporately as an organizational value to be shared throughout the organization. TQM is viewed as the next step, involving a movement beyond organization-wide procedures and standards, and encompasses a wider definition underpinned by wide scale employee involvement and participation.

In ETL's quality guide, Quality is defined as:

- fitness for purpose (in relation to the external customer) and
- conformance to requirement (as an internal definition).

According to the guide:

> "The first definition – *FITNESS FOR PURPOSE* – is used in our customer contacts and emphasizes the importance of discovering both the expressed and implied needs and expectations of the market. When these are mapped out, they are expressed in precise terms and are then included in our specifications. We then use – *CONFORMANCE TO REQUIREMENTS* – as our internal definition."

This definition is underpinned by the following statements made by ETL (statements are taken from the company's quality guide, "Ericsson Quality for the 1990s"):

- Ericsson stands for total Quality.
- Quality is judged by the "customer", not by the supplier. This is true of internal, as well as external customers.
- Our understanding of customer needs and the faultless functioning of our products are lasting factors which ensure the development and future of our Company.
- Customers shall come to ERICSSON because of the quality of our products and services.
- Quality is everyone's responsibility.

These statements are supported at the very highest level and signed by the Managing Director of ETL.

The Quality Policy is supported by a number of guiding principles which are said to drive quality at ETL. The principles are as follows:

- The ERICSSON name stands for Total Quality. Quality is everyone's responsibility. Everyone shall be made aware of this.
- Satisfied customers and the faultless functioning of our products are the surest signs of total quality.
- Quality in our daily work ensures that our performance is up to standard and adequate for the recipient.
- Total quality management of our Company's greatest asset – its people – is of vital importance.
- Quality objectives shall be formulated, audited, reviewed and followed up.
- Preventative measures and the elimination of defects shall be given first priority.
- Product quality shall be as important as costs and accurate delivery.

Five basic strategies for quality at ETL, aimed at securing a common approach are also cited.

Focusing on the Customer "We focus on the customer's needs and always act with the good of the customer in mind. This applies to all of our customers, internal as well as external. Our responsibility does not cease with the delivery of a product or service; we always support our customers."

Prevention "Prevention stresses the importance of doing it right first time. We do not achieve quality by screening, but by building quality into every product and process. The processes which generate our products are developed for stability and to give a minimum of variation. This is true for services as well as products."

Zero Defects "Zero defects means striving for faultless results. A failure rate is never acceptable. There always is a more cost effective way of producing better quality. We are continually seeking such improvements. Each incremental improvement we make brings us closer to zero defects."

Long-Term Thinking Long-term thinking stresses the unceasing nature of our work to improve our products and processes. Our long-term quality strategy allows us to adapt our operations to the changing demands of the market and to satisfy our customers, which is the very basis of long-term profitability.

Everyone's Full Participation This strategy creates conditions which allow every individual to take responsibility for the quality of his/her own work and then ensures that this responsibility is assumed. This calls for everyone's full participation in the improvement process. Only when everyone is actively involved in quality work can we achieve total operational quality. Thus the quality guide, which is available throughout the company, makes the link between Involvement and Total Quality. Some interviewees, however, felt that the organization had some way still to go before these strategies were fully achieved. For example, an interviewee stated that cutting costs within the organization sometimes overrides the strategy of focusing on the customer, although they did feel that the organization was in general, customer responsive. Another interviewee also described the organization as "reactive" and felt that the proactivity required for prevention was not yet in place across the company. These views were in contrast to one interviewee's response that they felt much progress had been made towards achieving zero defects. The quality awards such as ISO 9000 and EQA were also seen by the interviewee as useful milestones to reaching the long-term goal of quality in a time of recession which may encourage shorter-term reactions.

In addition to quality values, the key organizational values include respect, perseverance, and professionalism. These can be found in the overall Ericsson group statement of shared values, not just in ETL. Despite the relevance of these values to the aims of Total Quality and equal opportunities, it was not evident during the case study, that this connection had formerly been made.

Quality is organized around multi-functional teams on a limited time span which focus primarily on major issues.

The approach is not viewed as being pervasive, that is, the extent to which quality is active across the whole organization is limited. Several interviewees were unable to identify any quality teams operating in their area of work.

Quality Improvement Teams operate within the Cellular Division, each of which has a Facilitator selected by Section Heads nominating people. During interviews, it was estimated that the number of male facilitators was greater than the number of female facilitators.

Facilitators are sent on a four day course which includes

training in developing facilitator and communication skills, and tools and techniques for quality improvement.

Benchmarking is seen as a key measure of whether continuous improvement is occurring in the organization. However, one manager felt that benchmarking as a way of measuring TQ performance had the wrong profile in the division. One interviewee suggested that benchmarking was sometimes confused with key business measurements, which would obviously help an organization in benchmarking. It was suggested that there is some dissatisfaction and confusion amongst employees as to what benchmarking is, what benchmarks are and what key business measurements are. It was pointed out that Ericsson management have set a series of measurements that it believes will increase customer satisfaction.

A range of tools are provided through training which enable the quality improvement teams and process to work. Specific problem identification and analysis tools include pareto analysis, scatter diagrams and histograms. A range of tools are also used for the management process. These include brainstorming, affinity diagrams, tree diagrams, problem identification and solving tools, and process management tools. Measurement tools used include key performance indicators, cost analysis, activity based costing, and performance appraisal.

Total Quality Management: Case-Study Examples

The following illustrates two Divisional approaches to the implementation of Total Quality Management within ETL.

(1) Quality in the Public Systems Division   In the Public Systems Division, the organization for Total Quality is headed by a Total Quality Management steering committee. The committee is made up of senior management, which oversees a number of sub-groups. Each sub-group has a client manager who is also a member of the steering committee as well as a leader. The client manager communicates needs to the sub-group leader. These needs, which are linked to the business strategy, become the terms of reference for the sub-group. The leader presents the needs to the sub-group who brainstorm ideas for projects which will address the needs. The project ideas are presented to the

client manager who goes back to the steering committee to sell the ideas, which are either accepted (in which case a project is started) or rejected.

In addition to the steering committee, quality improvement teams operate, overseen by line managers in collaboration with the Total Quality Support Manager. Facilitators for these teams are selected by Section Heads and involvement is voluntary.

(2) Quality in the Cellular Division In the Cellular Division, training for quality co-ordinators is a five-day course spread out over a period of time to give an overview of what quality is about and how it can help each individual as well as each department. It works through processes and helps to find flaws in the processes of each department.

One viewpoint of the quality training shows how a fall in an individual's feeling of involvement with the issues of quality can occur. In one instance, a woman had experienced some problems fully engaging in training due to the technical nature of the material presented.

According to three interviewees, in the past, the Cellular Division had to face business problems which meant that quality was not regarded as the primary overriding issue. However they felt that quality is now being focused on far more and that this shift is reflected in the number of customer surveys now being carried out.

One manager stated that quality in the Cellular Division currently means providing quality products to customers and quality of service.

ETL's "total" approach to quality was interpreted by interviewees as being successful from point one and throughout the whole process, rather than being successful simply because a problem has been rectified.

The interviewees in general felt that the Cellular Division emphasizes the importance of a procedure approach to Quality Management. One view expressed suggested there was an implicit need to work to a set standard.

Interview results showed that a key element of Total Quality within the Cellular Division is the gearing of effort towards customer service, underlying the organizational value of meeting customer requirements and being responsive. One interviewee explained that the responsibility for the customer facing department for 1993, is to go out into the customer base and ask customers what they think about the organization, their strengths and weaknesses. The results of these will then be analysed and a series of projects set up, some to be cross-functional.

ETL: The Future Challenges of Total Quality Management

Some current problems associated with the drive towards TQM were highlighted during the seven interviews. Currently, ETL is undergoing a process of change in the area of TQM and a new policy is about to be implemented. Thus interviewees were expressing views in relation to past, present and future approaches to TQM. Problems highlighted included:

- problems are experienced with cascading the message of TQM down throughout the organization;
- problems are experienced in ensuring that all employees feel quality is their responsibility;
- problems are experienced in overcoming the view by some employees that TQM is a short-term project, rather than a long-term strategy.

However, the interviewees also described initiatives already being undertaken to overcome the above problems. These included the commencement of training for TQM to more efficiently communicate its values. Suggestions were also made by interviewees of ways in which they felt such problems could be overcome and progress towards achieving TQM could be improved. These included:

- ETL needs to recognize that there are different motivating factors for different people;
- there needs to be a rebalancing of training in people man-agement, particularly where some managers are people managers and others are cost managers;
- the company needs to build further on the strength of working in multi-functional groups;

- the company needs to actively pursue promoting TQ internally, e.g. with a handbook of tools and techniques, training, awareness days;
- employees need to know more about the competitive achievements of ETL in order to promote the idea of feeling committed to the mission and values of the company;
- clarity is needed about the values, strategy and role of quality and this needs to be communicated effectively;
- a more responsive approach to employee participation by senior managers is required. This could be brought about, according to some interviewees through a greater level of listening from senior management to ideas from lower down in the organization.

ETL: Total Quality Management – A Summary

With the achievement of ISO 9000 certification, the TQ policy has taken on a wider agenda and now focuses on customer service as well as quality and is now TQM. Quality is now a core organizational value. It was apparent during interviews within two ETL divisions that differences in the approach taken to TQM exist within the organization. This may reflect differing organizational subcultures, funding resources, budgets and size. Despite the progress TQ and TQM have already made within ETL, the need to further develop interfunctionality and involvement was stated. The latter need included developing wider commitment to TQM at both senior and lower levels in the organizational hierarchy.

ETL: Positive Action and Total Quality Management – The Involvement Gap

Despite the increasing emphasis on involvement and "people" in ETL's approach to TQM, a formal link between equal opportunities and TQM has not been made. However, some interviewees felt strongly that the values of equal opportunities complemented those of TQM and would help to raise employee involvement. Further development towards harmonizing these two objectives may help ETL to increase commitment to TQM and encourage interfunctionality. Ways in which development in this way may take place would be to use the guidelines of equal opportunity policies to ensure a better representation of women in team leader and facilitator positions.

British Telecommunications plc (BT)

BT: Background Information

BT is the UK's largest telecommunications company providing network services and equipment for personal and business communications as well as worldwide networks (see Figure 5.4 for organizational structure and markets). The Telecommunications Act (1984) abolished BT's exclusive privilege to run telecommunications systems and introduced the requirement of licensing for all UK telecommunications operators. In addition to licences granted to BT, Mercury and Kingston-upon-Hull were also granted public operator licences.

Under its operating licence, BT is required to provide telecommunications services to virtually the whole of the UK. The company is also specifically required to provide rural services, emergency services, directory enquiries and public payphone services.

Interviews were carried out in the areas of Quality Management, Personnel and Equal Opportunities. Specifically, managers were interviewed who had direct involvement with a recent BT initiative entitled "Involving Everyone". This initiative was designed to increase commitment and involvement across the organization in Total Quality Management and was introduced in 1985.

Since BT has become a public limited company, much of its activity is driven by the profit motive and external factors such as the share price, government regulation, competition and the current recession.

BT's goal, summed up in its vision of the future is "to become the most successful worldwide telecommunications group."

This is translated into a mission as follows:

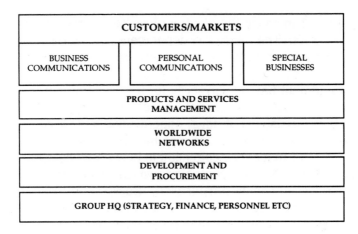

Figure 5.4 BT – Corporate Organization and Markets

- to provide world-class telecommunications and information products and services;
- to develop and exploit networks, within the UK and overseas, so that BT can: meet customer requirements; sustain growth in the earnings of the group on behalf of the shareholders; make a fitting contribution to the community in which BT conduct their business.

This is underpinned by a set of "BT values":

- we put our customers first (supported by a communications initiative called "Putting Customers First");
- we are professional;
- we respect each other;
- we work as a team;
- we are committed to continuous improvement.

BT: Corporate Approach to Positive Action and Equal Opportunities

The equal opportunities policy within BT was introduced during the mid-1970s and developed during the mid-1980s.

Through the company's commitment to Opportunity 2000, BT

also aims to increase the number of women in management by the year 2000. The Personnel department has overall responsibility for the implementation of the equality policy, together with the equal opportunity advisory group. The Headquarters Personnel department has responsibility for the strategy and policy of equal opportunities. Personnel Services have responsibility for the day to day issues of equal opportunities and Divisional line personnel are responsible for implementing the policy.

In 1991, BT made their commitment to the National campaign, Opportunity 2000. The campaign, was launched by the independent British charity organization, "Business in the Community", with the support of the British Government. The campaign encourages and supports companies such as BT in their aims to increase the "quality and quantity of women's participation in the workforce" by the year 2000.

Since the launch of the Opportunity 2000 initiative, BT now has a manager responsible for achieving the goals of Opportunity 2000. It also now has a member of the Management Board accountable for equal opportunities. This has given equal opportunities within BT far greater visibility and a regular report of its progress is now made to the main Board. The monitoring data collected is now used to make projections and identify trends. It is also used to make targets or estimates of where the company wishes to be in the future. In this way, equal opportunities monitoring information is used both at a corporate and local level.

BT's equal opportunity policy is extensive in its inclusion of working towards equality of opportunity in the areas of gender, race, marital status, disability and religion.

In recent years a growing number of women have reached management positions within BT. However, top management remains heavily dominated by men, and women are predominantly in the lower levels of the company, particularly in telephone operator positions.

Positive Action and Equal Opportunity Initiatives

Possibly one of the furthest reaching initiatives BT have taken towards the achievement of its equality goals was becoming part of the Opportunity 2000 campaign. Certainly, involvement in the campaign has succeeded in lifting the profile of equal opportunities within the organization.

In addition to the influence of Opportunity 2000, several other initiatives in pursuit of the equality goals have been launched by BT.

(1) Monitoring Statistical analysis and monitoring mechanisms have been implemented in order that an overall picture of the position of individual groups within BT can be understood. The records are used for contributing information to the formulation of policy and new positive actions. To this end, information on gender and disability is already held within the organization. A monitoring exercise on ethnicity has been undertaken, as has an audit in the area of appraisals and internal promotion. Qualitative information in the area of equal opportunities is gathered through "CARE", the attitudinal survey of BT employees.

(2) Networking A network of equal opportunity advisors within BT has been established. Members of the network meet and share their experiences in implementing the equality policy. A senior management equal opportunities committee also exists that consults with line personnel in developing strategies and plans.

(3) Child Care Although a child care policy has not been implemented throughout the company, some child care subsidies or remuneration have arisen from local initiatives. Currently the implementation of a child care initiative within BT is under consideration, including an on-site crèche.

(4) Recruitment Recruitment drives are initiated to attract women graduates through promotional literature and visits to universities. Such drives are aimed in particular at non-traditional areas of female employment.

(5) Flexi-Work Organization Opportunities to job share and work part-time are available in most areas of the company and the option to work flexi-time is available to all employees. Almost all job-sharers within BT are women as are most, but not all, part-time workers. The number of job sharers within the company, although boosted by the initiatives of Opportunity 2000 remain low. Flexi-work is taken up by most people within the organization regardless of gender. Research is also currently being undertaken within BT into the development of home-working, and a number of areas already offer tele-working.

(6) Training   Although no specific company wide training on equal opportunities has taken place within recent years in BT, interviewees felt that equal opportunities was taken into consideration when formalizing general training courses. This was illustrated through the training undertaken for two company wide programmes, the Leadership Programme and the Preparation for Management Programme. It was felt that equal opportunities was reflected in both these programmes by addressing the stated BT value of respecting each other as an individual.

Some equal opportunities training has been undertaken in areas where a need arose and for some personnel staff. However, it was indicated that such training had been undertaken on an ad hoc basis and it was difficult to determine the number of staff that had undergone such training. A major plan for the current year is the implementation of equal opportunities awareness training for all employees.

In the area of recruitment, both internal and external, selectors are fully trained in assessment techniques, an element of which includes equal opportunities.

Positive action training for women in the field of personal development have been run within BT since the late 1980s. For example, BT run a women's development course at Cranfield College. This is aimed at second level management who have been identified as having the potential to progress their careers to a higher level within the organization. A second such course is offered to more senior managers. About 40 women a year attend these training courses aimed at meeting women's developmental needs. A third course, run totally by BT, is aimed at first line women managers.

Internal conversion initiatives such as those encouraging women to enter the field of engineering have also been run within BT.

BT: Positive Action and Equal Opportunities: The Future

Numerous initiatives have already been taken within BT in pursuit of equal opportunities that have made far reaching accomplishments within the organization. However, several further action points were highlighted that was felt would move the organization closer to its aim of reaching equal opportunities. These included:

- further education and training to heighten awareness of equal opportunities throughout the organization;
- improve the implementation and opportunity throughout the organization of taking career breaks;
- improve policies on child care;
- heighten awareness through education on how flexible forms of working can operate and be beneficial in various functional areas;
- increase the amount of equal opportunity specific training throughout the organization.

BT: Positive Action and Equal Opportunities: Barriers to Future Policy Aims

During interviews, a number of barriers to the achievement of the aims of equal opportunities and the implementation of the initiatives stated above were highlighted. These included the following:

- suspicion concerning the effect of equal opportunities on job security: At the time of the launch of the BT's commitment to Opportunity 2000, there was a positive feeling within the company towards the aims of equal opportunity. However, evidence was found during interviews that during the current period of recession that has brought down-sizing to streamline the organization, equal opportunities and the current ethnic monitoring exercise have come to be regarded with suspicion by many employees as constituting quotas and therefore a threat to job security. Some people were worried that they would be pushed out in favour of minority groups.
- equality being regarded as a Personnel issue: Data collected during the interviews suggested that currently, equal opportunities is perceived as a personnel issue by many employees, rather than a company wide issue. It is the

aim within BT that this barrier be overcome by increased openness of the issues central to equality, by making everyone aware of their responsibility to equality and the consequences of not achieving equality. Through increased communication and training, emphasis will be placed on personal responsibility for achieving equality.

- lack of understanding throughout the organization as to what equality means: It was suggested that this barrier could be overcome through making "risky" appointments and ensuring that women are represented at all levels of responsibility.
- lack of resources devoted to promoting equal opportunities;
- existing procedures and policies such as entry criteria for certain posts and grades;
- lack of a proactive approach to equal opportunities;
- the "macho" or strongly male image of company;
- equal opportunities is regarded by many employees as being the "flavour of the month", that is, a temporary initiative: It was suggested that this barrier could be overcome by making achievement of equal opportunities part of the managers personal objectives, thereby making it a business issue.

BT: Positive Action/Equal Opportunities – A Summary

BT have succeeded in making significant progress in their pursuit of equal opportunities through the implementation of several equality initiatives.

However, objectives exist to further progress towards equality, specifically through flexible working, heightening company-wide awareness and increasing the understanding of the policy. In particular, interviews highlighted the fact that seeing equality as a Personnel issue has caused some problems in raising awareness and responsibility for equality throughout the company.

BT: Corporate Approach to Total Quality Management

Total Quality was introduced within BT in 1985. Its aim was to support BT in a more dynamic, deregulated environment as a private business entity. According to one interviewee:

"BT used to be a paternalistic, hierarchical organization,"

and that:

"BT's problem is one of transition from old to new."

Total Quality was introduced as part of BT's drive to shake off the shackles of being a large bureaucratic monopoly and to become economically successful in the commercial market. Since 1986, various reorganizations have taken place within BT which have been described as undermining Total Quality efforts. One view expressed this as:

"there was no continuity of drive due to changing senior management roles, organizational changes undermined it."

The biggest reorganization under the banner of "Project Sovereign" and the "Putting Customers First" initiative generated the new Total Quality set of values.

The quality strategy at BT is defined as follows:

BT's goal is to achieve and sustain quality in everything it does. Total Quality is the strategic means by which BT is changing its culture to achieve the attitude of Putting Customers First. (*1001 Facts: a pocket guide to BT*, 1991)

According to the documentation in "Putting Customers First":

Our success depends on our people. The values that underpin the way we work together and the way we deal with the outside world are therefore absolutely fundamental to our progress. Applying these values to everything we do, and demanding the same of our colleagues, is the key to a more successful company and a more fulfilling job.

Thus, the BT literature suggests there is a link between involvement and success. This has been more recently supported by a company wide programme entitled "Involving Everyone".

Organization for Total Quality Management

BT has established Quality Councils, operating at all levels, to champion the principles of Total Quality. Team-based quality improvement teams are set up within functional areas to work on quality issues. This process is underpinned by the quality strategy.

According to the Chairman, the company must:

- drive quality from the top;
- pursue excellence in customer service;
- support BT people in achieving Total Quality;
- set and achieve world-best standards of management.

The third point on this list suggests the need for total involvement in the organization of Total Quality.

Quality Measures

Customer service is seen as a key measure for Total Quality.

A twice-yearly report is produced which covers payphones, the telephone service, service provision to both business and residential customers, network reliability, operator services and private circuit provision. This report involves the presentation of Quality of Service Statistics. An example from the 1991 report is that 95 percent of all UK public payphones are working at any one time.

Further measures include:

- cost reduction;
- product defects.

Tools for Quality Improvement

(1) The Leadership Programme   This initiative involved training sessions developing leadership skills to help ensure that teams succeed under the pressures of tight time scales and resources.

(2) The "Involving Everyone" programme The "Involving Everyone" Initiative at BT, introduced recently, commences

with a one-day awareness/training session. It is the aim that each employee should undergo the training which covers:

- the BT values and the BT mission;
- a statement on the difficulties the company is in and the "current situation", e.g. the effects of the recession;
- an introduction to Total Quality tools: brainstorming; consensus reaching.

Once all employees within a work unit have attended the one-day training session, this is followed up by a series of planned, ongoing activities in the workplace.

Employee Perceptions of Total Quality Management

A wide range of views were expressed about Total Quality Management at BT. The following are the common perceptions expressed by the majority of interviewees:

- the ability of an employee to take on board the Total Quality Management message depended on how ingrained older values were. Many interviewees feel that there are still a significant number who have worked in BT for a long time and either find it hard to change, or simply do not wish to do so;
- people were very "fired up" about Total Quality Management at the beginning;
- workshops were generally well delivered (with one or two exceptions) and the messages clear;
- Total Quality Management was seen very much as a top-down approach, led by senior managers;
- Total Quality Management was a business-driven initiative;
- there was considerable scope to improve the way supplier-buyer relations were managed and Total Quality Management improvement processes could provide the right approach;
- involvement in Total Quality Management was patchy and interviewees have found people in BT even today who haven't been on their first workshop.

BT: The Future Challenges of Total Quality Management

It was the perception amongst interviewees that TQM within BT is currently experiencing some difficulties. Many interviewees felt that:

- "Total Quality Management has gone flat"; "there were a lot of QIPs [Quality Improvement Programmes] at first but they weren't really followed through";
- there has been a lack of employee involvement in QIPs;
- team briefings, much in evidence at first, have begun, in many cases, to disappear or have turned into monthly house-keeping meetings;
- there are still many examples of QIPs which are being successfully run and managed;
- Project Sovereign is viewed by many employees as a great underminer of Total Quality Management. The huge amount of rumour and effects on morale of redundancies according to one interviewee: "put Total Quality Management on the back burner, and it's been there ever since."

Several interviewees feel that many of the Total Quality Management values (including continuous improvement and problem solving) are now embedded in their daily working lives. In other words they are "living" Total Quality Management. This implies that, although many procurement people may not be using formal mechanisms such as QIPs, the basic process of continuous improvement, and even some of the improvement processes may be being used. However, this is being done on an informal and ad-hoc basis depending on how much an individual or unit has "bought in" to the Total Quality Management ideology.

A large number of interviewees also expressed the view that many colleagues held back from making any improvements suggestions which might in some way leave them vulnerable to redundancy or becoming marginalized in their unit. At the other extreme, examples were given where managers had initiated changes which could demonstrate cost savings (thus justifying or reinforcing a manager's position) but which led to problems elsewhere.

A number of recommendations were generated during the

interviews which may possibly overcome the present challenges of Total Quality at BT:

- elevate the whole "Involving Everyone" programme in terms of the company's priorities so that the organization can really "live Total Quality Management';
- more attendance/involvement at workshops;
- need a more unified ownership of Total Quality Management at a senior level;
- set a "house style" for Total Quality Management;
- more resources for supporting quality;
- Total Quality is needed at a strategic level;
- involvement workshops need a well-directed project office, strong personalities driving it through, people should know why they're attending.

BT: Total Quality Management – A Summary

Since the introduction of TQM into BT in the mid-1980s, several initiatives have been undertaken in pursuit of the goals of TQ. The company now has an overall strategy for achieving quality and mechanisms are in place to measure its progress and initiatives, such as the "Leadership" and "Involving Everyone" programmes to introduce the values and tools of TQ. However, it was highlighted that gaining widespread involvement to and understanding of the BT issues remains problematic. This may be due, in part to the number of subcultures existing within BT, and the perceived patchy approach to training for TQ. However, these problems, it was felt could be overcome through expansion of the "Involving Everyone" programme, increased top level commitment and increased resources made available for quality.

BT: Positive Action and Total Quality Management – The Involvement Gap

There was some overlap between the values of equal opportunities and TQ, but no explicit action has been undertaken within

BT to harmonize some of the objectives in order to increase the effectiveness of the two policies.

Indeed, interviews indicated that the development of women's networks that have evolved within BT during the past four years have helped women to feel more involved within the company. It was also perceived that the communication of the aims of Opportunity 2000 and BT's commitment to this has helped women to feel more positive about the company.

Feedback from interviewees suggested that women have been able to take on board more easily the values of the BT "Involving Everyone" initiative. It was suggested this was as a result of women being positioned more within customer facing jobs rather than the more customer removed roles.

Some of the future challenges BT face concerns employees' full involvement in the values of TQ. Similarly, a problem facing the achievement of equal opportunities objectives was the widespread understanding and commitment of employees at all levels. The organization may in the future benefit from the application and harmonization of many of the values of the equal opportunities and TQ policies.

6

Bridging the Involvement Gap: Conclusions and Recommendations

Conclusions

The overall objectives of this study were two-fold:

- to review the progress and approach of European tele-communication companies to equality and quality;
- to explore the link between positive action/equal opportunities and Total Quality Management.

Within the context of improving organizational competitiveness, the study reviewed the progress and approach of European telecommunication companies to both equality and quality. The findings showed that of the three organizations that established their equality policies between the mid 1970s and early 1980s, considerable progress has been achieved in this area. Despite such improvements, however, the companies continue to strive towards the objectives of:

- increasing the number of women in management;
- increasing training for diversifying women's skills;
- increasing the number of women in technical and traditionally male jobs;
- increasing organization wide awareness and responsibility for equality;
- improving provisions to enable women to more easily combine career and family.

In working towards these objectives, companies also continue to find themselves faced with barriers, some of which have been long-standing. They include:

- suspicion concerning the effect of equal opportunities on job security in the current economic and in some cases political climate;
- equality being regarded as a Personnel issue;
- lack of understanding throughout the organization as to what equality means;
- lack of resources devoted to developing equal opportunities;
- cultural influences from society on the traditional role of women.

It is suggested that a reason for the continued existence of these barriers is the failure of equality policies in the past, to synchronize their objectives with the strategic objectives of the organization.

In the area of quality too, five of the six organizations had made considerable progress towards the achievement of TQM objectives.

The case studies indicated that TQM was sometimes received differently within separate parts of the organization and levels of commitment to the values of TQM, varied. Some concern was also expressed within companies as to how commitment and progress towards TQM could be, in some cases, maintained, and in others, improved. A presupposition of the study was that a sustained and improved commitment could be ensured through employee involvement.

The concept of involvement was also central to the study's second objective, that of exploring the link between positive action/equal opportunities and TQM. This was because involvement is a theme which is common to the literature on Total Quality Management and equal opportunities. Such commonality generated an interesting hypothesis:

- that the involvement of employees which underpins the Total Quality Management philosophy, and which is lacking in many companies implementing TQM, may be increased through the development of a positive-action led, equality-driven approach to Total Quality.

The findings of this research, though only at an exploratory level, strongly suggest that such a link exists and that, by integrating the practices of equal opportunities into the fabric of Total Quality Management, the goals of both Total Quality Management and positive action can be furthered. Indeed such an integration would contribute to the achievement of the commercial objectives of the company.

The initial findings suggest that a generalistic approach to involvement in Total Quality Management, which does not take account of the needs of diverse organizational groups, will be of limited success, particularly in organizations where there is scope to improve equality of opportunity. The companies in the survey are at different stages of Total Quality Management and equal opportunities. Some working environments are viewed as more equal than others. However, in all cases there was a recognition that the needs of certain groups within the organization (by gender, age or functional background) had not always been reflected in the framework for Total Quality, and that this might well affect personal commitment and involvement among those groups.

The conclusions reached in the report are thus three-fold, that:

1   equality objectives are likely to be more effectively implemented if synchronized with overall organizational strategic objectives;
2   organizations adopting TQM will benefit with a focus on issues of involvement at a greater level. The diversity of the workforce needs to be recognized, and TQM should be designed to bring out the best in the diversity. It is argued that quality awards such as ISO 9000 or the European Quality Awards should not be viewed as the end of the Total Quality road, but be assessed in relation to achieving involvement from women and men employees;
3   a commonality exists between the goals of positive action/equal opportunities and TQM through involvement. Hence a linked approach, through an equality-driven TQM

philosophy, represents an opportunity for improving the success of both TQM and equality policies.

Recommendations

The results of the study highlight certain possible options for organizational action and for achieving a synchronized approach towards TQM and positive action.

The current options represent only possible areas of exploration, analysis and further research. They do not constitute a detailed programme for change. It is envisaged that a programme for change will arise only after a detailed assessment of the identified option. In order to facilitate such assessments, concrete criteria have to be formulated in order to gauge success and to fully establish the link between positive action and the success of TQM.

Result 1: Traditional appointment of quality group facilitators and leaders is tied to the traditional hierarchical structure of the organization

Equality-Driven Total Quality could:

- provide specific training for women in TQM skills;
- emphasize cross training for women in developing leadership/facilitator skills/ business skills;
- emphasize cross training in new technological skills which TQM supports and supports TQM;
- promote career development of women to enable them to have a "holistic view" (which underpins successful TQM);
- develop procedures for selection and recruitment similar to those in the formal hierarchy;
- establish a procedure for communicating TQ posts including style, communication of the advertisements, presentation and distribution of the advertisements and awareness training to encourage women to apply;
- establish selection procedures which follow positive action guidelines;

- establish appeals procedures which follow equal opportunity guidelines;
- encourage peer group selection in areas where a particular group of women is high in number;
- generate new forms of work organization which do not inhibit flexi-workers or part-time workers from becoming TQ leaders or participants.

Lesson: *Positive action needs to be built into the organizational framework for TQM.*

Result 2: Little or no mechanisms exist within the current TQM framework to support new forms of work organization such as flexi-working, tele-working and part-time working

Equality-Driven Total Quality could:

- ensure that flexi-workers are not excluded from quality improvement teams by ensuring times of team meetings and training sessions do not conflict with the needs of flexi-workers or tele-workers. The overall argument is that the drawbacks of flexi-working found to exist in traditional hierarchy, e.g. invisibility, should not occur in TQM;
- encourage the redesigning of TQM to reflect the needs of part-time and contract workers and value their input. Such redesign should be built explicitly into the TQM policy;
- promote investment in technology that improves communication for tele-workers and others working away from the workplace;
- raise awareness throughout the organization of the different needs and value of the different groups of workers.

Lesson: *People consist of different groups within the organization with different needs and values that need to be explicitly acknowledged and addressed.*

Result 3: Training design does not reflect the goals of equal opportunities

Equality-Driven Total Quality could:

- involve equality experts in the design of training material and delivery system and in the selection of participants;
- collect data about who is and who is not attending courses and on whose initiative it is that people go on training courses;
- ensure opportunity for feedback on the quality of courses and in particular the relevance and accessibility of the courses;
- make training a quality improvement issue;
- organize training delivery to be flexible to meet differing needs, e.g. open learning packages for tele-workers and part-time workers;
- relate training material more to the interests of diverse groups.

Lesson: *Training should be accessible and relevant to the diverse groups in the organization.*

Result 4: Different divisions, functions and roles within the organization receive TQM differently

Equality-Driven Total Quality could:

- ensure training that is sensitive to: functional area; age; gender;
- ensure the development of cross-functional teams;
- promote involvement in areas where commitment to the TQM values is low.

Lesson: *A uniform approach to the implementation of TQM does not always reflect and take into account the diversity of people within the organization.*

Result 5: No established evidence of the potential benefits of the link between equal opportunities/positive action and TQM through involvement currently exists

Equality-Driven Total Quality could:

- benchmark against best practice (that is, what are other successful equality-driven total quality organizations doing and what measures are they using?);

- measure the benefits of the link through surveys and feed-back;
- analyse current involvement levels and TQ initiatives by gen-der, age and function, e.g. level of contribution to suggestion schemes;
- set targets to increase involvement across different groups, e.g. increase in number of suggestions from specific groups;
- build equal opportunities into the TQM managerial perfor-mance appraisal;
- build equal opportunities into the fabric of the core TQM values and policy, that is combine the equal opportunities and TQM values and emphasize the overlap in particular in the area of involvement;
- raise the awareness of the link at Board level;
- move beyond narrow approaches such as ISO 9000.

Lesson: *Further research is required to firmly establish the potential benefits of building positive action into TQM programmes.*

7

Future Research and Action

The survey results indicate scope for improving positive action and Total Quality Management programmes in the telecommunications sector through a conscious synchronization in the implementation of two related, but currently separately-pursued, corporate policies. The investigation of the reduction or elimination of the "involvement gap', defined as the shortfall in success of many organizational approaches to TQM, associated particularly with a lack of employee participation and commitment to the management philosophy, provides a major area requiring further action-oriented research. The survey shows that a general lack of co-ordination, between TQM and equal opportunities divisions in the telecommunications companies, generally manifests itself in:

- current practices relating to TQM that do not explicitly take into account the needs, expertise and career aspirations of women employees;
- selection of TQ leaders and facilitators in a hierarchical structure which makes it difficult for women to attain these positions;
- a lack of training programmes in transferable business and personal development skills that make women (and men) effective and confident contributors to TQM group activities;
- an absence of mechanisms to evaluate or support new forms of work organization such as flexi-work, part-time work or tele-work, that allow women (and men) to combine potentially a challenging career with domestic commitments.

The findings of the pilot survey were substantiated by the

results of a workshop that was held in Brussels on February 16, 1993. It was attended by management and union, quality and equality representatives from the survey companies, by the representatives of PTTI and by members of DG-XIII (Directorate-General – Telecommunications, Information Industries & Innovation) and DG-V of the EC. One of the aims of the workshop was to present the overall findings of the survey to relevant partners. The other aim was to reach a consensus regarding priorities and sequences of action in future research and work programmes in this field.

In reaching such a consensus, a Total Quality tool, namely paired comparison, was used. The tool is a method of gaining group consensus on the order of priority of a list of action points which appear to have equal importance.

The five major results of the study were used as a basis for determining the priority of focus of future research and action. The study results were combined with suggested action that could help improve performance and results in the workplace. The study results were as follows, that:

- traditional appointment of quality group facilitators and leaders is tied to the traditional hierarchical structure of the organization. As men were found to be in the majority of management positions, levels where many of the quality group facilitators are drawn from, this may pose barriers to women becoming facilitators. This potentially may affect women's involvement with TQM;
- little or no mechanisms to support new forms of work organization such as flexi-working and part-time working were found within the TQM framework. This meant that potentially, part-time or flexi-workers, the majority of whom are women, may be excluded from full involvement in the TQM process and culture;
- training design does not consistently reflect the goals of equal opportunities. It is suggested that design and selection of participants should be addressed to ensure full involvement and relevance of training to staff;
- different divisions, functions and roles within the organization receive TQM differently. This result suggests that action should be taken to take account of the diverse needs of

Results of preliminary research on EO/PA and TQM	Paired comparison score	Action	Priority/ rating
Selection of TQ leaders and facilitators	35	Address	4
Little or no mechanisms to support new forms of work organisation eg flexi-work, tele-work, part-time work	15	Develop	6
Training design does not reflect the goals of EO	41	Re-design	2
Different divisions, functions and roles within the organisation receive TQM differently	35	Customise	4
No established evidence of the potential benefits of the link between EO/PA and TQM through involvement	**66**	**Establish and measure**	**1**
Diversification of skills	39	Develop	3

Table 7.1   Priority Areas for Future Research and Action

different groups and individuals within the organization and customize the implementation of TQM appropriately;
• no established evidence of the potential benefits of the link between equal opportunities/positive action and TQM through involvement was found. The results of this study indicate that involvement levels may be increased by incorporating positive action into TQM programmes. Further research and action is required to determine the benefit this may have for achieving TQM objectives.

A final area, that of skills diversification was added by the workshop group as an area for discussion regarded as relevant and important in light of the study's result that the telecommunication companies' demand for technical skills was increasing.

Table 7.1 illustrates the list of results and action used within the paired comparison exercise. It shows the scores that the workshop participants assigned to each area and the priority for action that resulted. With a score of 66, the workshop participants felt that the main area of priority for future research and action lay with trying to establish and measure the benefits of linking positive action with TQM programmes through involvement.

The challenge of how equality and quality policies and programmes could be aligned in practice has now been taken up within a second European research programme being conducted by the authors within CENTRIM at the University of Brighton. The research team, who are working with a further nine European companies, are developing a model of Equality Driven Total Quality. The model will illustrate how alignment can be achieved, the organizational changes and management capabilities this will require and an analysis of the benefits resulting from alignment.

Bibliography

Bennis, W (1966) *Changing Organizations*, McGraw-Hill.

Bessant, J (1991) *Managing Advanced Manufacturing Technology – The Challenge of the Fifth Wave*, NCC Blackwell, Oxford.

Bessant, J, Caffyn, S, Gilbert, J, Harding, R, and Webb, S, (1994), *Rediscovering Continuous Improvement, Technovation*, vol. 14, no. 1, pp. 17–29.

Bessant, J; Levy, P; Ley, C; Smith, S & Tranfield, D (1991) *Coping with Chaos: Designing the Organization for Factory 2000*, paper presented to the Annual Conference of the Institute for Electrical Engineers, University of York, UK.

Bevort, F; Pedersen, J S; Sundbo, J, University of Roskilde, Denmark (1992) *Human Resource Management in Denmark*, Employee Relations, vol. 14, no. 4, pp. 6–20, MCB University Press.

Bos, A H (1971) lecture given at the IUC Congress, Czechoslovakia, (NPI), Zeist, Holland.

Brunstein, I (1992) *Human Resource Management in France*, Employee Relations, vol. 14, no. 4, pp. 53–70.

Carlisle, J & Parker, R (1989) *Beyond Negotiation*, John Wiley and Sons, New York.

Clarkson, P & Shaw, P (1992) *Human Relationships at Work in Organizations*, Journal of Management Education and Development, vol. 23, part 1, pp. 18–29.

Commission of the European Communities and PTTI (1988) *Telecommunications in Europe: Free Choice for the User in Europe's 1992 Market: The Challenge for the European Community*, European Perspective Series, Brussels, 1988.

Commission of the European Communities and PTTI (1991) *Evolution et Structures de l'Emploi dans les Telecommunications*, Principaux Resultats Eurostrategies, TURU.

Commission of the European Communities, COM (91) 511: *First Report on the Application of the Community Charter of the Fundamental Social Rights of Workers*.

Covey, S, (1993), *Principle Centred Leadership*, Simon and Schuster, London.

Crosby, P (1979) *Quality is Free*, McGraw-Hill, New York.

Deming, W E (1988) *Out of the Crisis*, MIT Centre for Advanced Engineering Study, Cambridge, Mass.

DG-XIII (September 1992) *Official Documents Community Telecommunications Policy*, Commission of the European Communities, Update DG XIII (92) 260–EN.

Directorate-General Employment Industrial Relations and Social Affairs (1991) *Women of the South in European Integration: Problems and Prospects*, Commission of the European Communities, Centre for Research on Women's Issues.

Directorate-General Employment, Industrial Relations and Social Affairs (1992) *Employment in Europe*, Commission of the European Communities, COM (92) 345.

Directorate-General for Employment, Industrial Relations and Social Affairs (March 1991) *Social Europe: Equal Opportunities for women and men*, Commission of the European Communities.

Foster, M., and Whittle, S., (1990), *The Quality Management Maze, Implementing TQM*, IFS Publications, Kempston 88.

Garrat, B., (1987), *The Learning Organisation*, Fontana Gauvin, A & Silvera, R: *French Report*, Women of Europe Supplements, no. 36.

Greiner, L (July–August 1972) Evolution and Revolution as Organizations Grow, *Harvard Business Review*.

Hayes, R. and Jaikumar, R., (1988), Manufacturing Crisis: New Technologies, Obsolete Organisations, *Harvard Business Review*, vol. 68.

Hofstede, G (1991) *Culture and Organizations: Software of the Mind*, Institute for Research on Intercultural Co-operation, University of Limburg at Maastricht, The Netherlands, McGraw-Hill.

Imai, M., (1986), *Kaizen: The Key To Japan's Competitive Success*, McGraw-Hill, New York.

Juran, J (1951) *Quality Control Handbook*, McGraw-Hill, New York.

Kearney, A T (1992) *Total Quality: Time to Take Off the Rose-Tinted Spectacles*, survey by A T Kearney and TQM Magazine, IFS, Kempston, UK.

Keynote (1992) *UK Telecommunications*.

Lamming, R & Bessant, J (1988) *Macmillan Dictionary of Business and Management*, Macmillan, Basingstoke.

Leavitt, H J; Dill, W R & Eyrin, H B (1973) *The Organizational World*, Harcourt Brace Jovanovich Inc, New York.

Lessem, R (1990) *Developmental Management: Principles of Holistic Business*, Basil Blackwell, Oxford.

——, (1992) *Total Quality Learning*, Basil Blackwell, Oxford.

Lievegoed, B J (1991) *Managing the Developing Organization*, Basil Blackwell, Oxford.

Mair, A, (1994), *Hondas Global Flexifactory Network*, International Journal of Operations and Production Management, vol. 14, no. 3, pp. 6–23.

Maruani, M (March 1992) *The Position of Women on the Labour Market: Trends and Developments in the 12 Member States of the European Community 1983–1990*.

McWhinney, W., (1993), *All Creative People Are Not Alike*, Creativity and

Innovation Management, vol. 2, no. 1, March, pp. 3–15.

Michele, M (Canada) (June 1–2 1992) *Struggling to take part: Women in the Telecommunications Industry*, from an International conference on Gender Technology and ethics, Sweden, pp. 161–73.

Mitter, S (1991) *Computer-aided Manufacturing and Women's Employment: A Global Critique of Post-Fordism*, paper presented at the Conference on Women, Work and Computerization, Helsinki, Finland, 30 June–2 July 1991.

Mohn, R (1981) *Success through Partnership – An Entrepreneurial Strategy*, Bantam Press, London.

Moss Kanter, R., (1983), *The Change Masters*, Simon and Schuster.

Nielson, R (1987) *Equality Between Women and Men in Danish Labour Law*.

Noam, E (1992) *Telecommunications in Europe*, Oxford: Oxford University Press.

Oakland, J (1989) *Total Quality Management*, Pitman, London.

OECD (1982) *Economic Survey of the UK (Organization for Economic Co-operation and Development)*, Paris.

Papalexandris, N (1992) *Human Resource Management in Greece*, Employee Relations, vol. 14, no. 4, pp. 38–52.

Pedler, M; Boydell, T & Burgoyne, J (1991) *The Learning Company*, McGraw Hill, London.

Price Waterhouse Cranfield Project (1991) *International Strategic Human Resource Management*, The Price Waterhouse Cranfield Project.

Revans, R (1980) *Action Learning – New Techniques for Management*, London, Bond & Briggs.

Roosevelt Thomas, R (1992) *Beyond Race and Gender*, Amacom (American Management Association).

Sang, R (1992) *Advocacy, Empowerment and Service Quality*, AMED Public Service Conference Papers.

Schein, E (1984) *Coming to a New Awareness of Organizational Culture*, Sloan Management Review.

——, (1985) *Organization Culture and Leadership*, Jossey Bass.

Schonberger, R, (1982), *Japanese Manufacturing Techniques: Nine Hidden Lessons in Simplicity*, The Free Press, New York.

Singh, I B (ed.) (1983) *Telecommunications in the Year 2000*, ABLEX Publishing Corporation, New Jersey.

Smeds, R (1994), *Managing Change Towards Lean Enterprises*, International Journal of Operations and Production Management, vol. 14, no. 3, pp. 66–82.

Taylor, P (October 15 1992) *Financial Times Survey*, UK.

Whittle, S; Smith, S; Tranfield, D & Foster, M (1992) *Total Quality and Change Management: Integrating Approaches for Organization Design*, paper presented at IEE Third International Conference: Factory 2000, University of York, IEE Conference Publication 359.

Womack, J P, Jones, D T, and Roos, D, (1990), *The Machine That Changed The World*, Rawson Associates, New York.

Index